Christine Izeki | Björn N

D1622819

111 Places
in Tokyo
That You
Shouldn't Miss

(111)

emons:

© Emons Verlag GmbH
All rights reserved
© for photographs: Björn Neumann and Christine Izeki, except:
place 3: Tono Magokoro Net (photo above and below);
place 7: Bamba Hotel;
place 11: Book and Bed Tokyo (photo above and below);
place 13: Tsutaya Electrics (photo above and below);
place 17: Jugetsudo;
place 30: inGOLF (photo above and below);
place 42: Kawanone (restaurant photo);
place 44: Maison Koichiro Kimura;
place 47: The Kurosawa (photo above and below);
place 55: Meguro Gajoen (photo above and below);
place 71: The Owl Cafe;
place 87: Tokyo Sewerage Museum 'Rainbow'
© Cover motif: depositphotos.com/vichly
English translation: John Sykes
Design: Eva Kraskes, based on a design
by Lübbeke | Naumann | Thoben
Maps: altancicek.design, www.altancicek.de
Printing and binding: CPI – Clausen & Bosse, Leck
Printed in Germany 2017
ISBN 978-3-7408-0024-6

Did you enjoy it? Do you want more?
Join us in uncovering new places around the world on:
www.111places.com

Foreword

At first sight Tokyo is not a beautiful city, but appears to be an impenetrable urban jungle. A mood like that in Sofia Coppola's film *Lost in Translation* is created by a grey sea of houses stretching to the horizon, masses of people that always seem to be in motion, and permanent background noise. Nevertheless, no one who takes on the challenge of exploring one of the world's biggest cities off the tourist track will be disappointed.

Often it is precisely the places that are hidden and not eye-catching that leave a lasting impression. Join us on a journey of discovery, tracking down little-known temples, tea houses and themed restaurants. Amongst the 111 places described in this book, you will find a few, from A for anime to Z for Zen, whose existence in Tokyo will probably come as a surprise.

Did you know, for example, that this city is extremely haunted, that there are clubs where passionate amateur bands get everyone rocking, and that Tokyo's boundaries also include rural areas that are wonderful places for hiking? Or why the Sanya quarter disappeared from the street map? Our 111 Places in Tokyo That You Shouldn't Miss will provide answers to these questions.

We, the author and photographer, have known each other for many years, ever since we hit on the crazy idea of studying Japanese language and culture in Hamburg. Although we were given gloomy forecasts for our careers, we have not abandoned our dream, and for many years now have lived in this city, which is a never-ending source of inspiration. We have often set off together with a camera, looking for interesting sights that have not yet been discovered for tourism. In this book we are pleased to present a selection of our favourite places.

111 Places

1___3331 Arts Chiyoda
Off to school

What is the meaning of the number 3331 in the name of this arts centre? Is it part of the address? Or a date? The answer is less banal, because the number stands for the concept of the institution, which appears, at first sight, to be a mixed-up array of things.

Once a middle school, it is now a place where people can take their offspring to a children's workshop, eat and drink in a café-bar, buy arts and crafts in a large number of shops, purchase cameras in the Lomo shop, look at exhibitions, browse around a few galleries of contemporary art, hire rooms for workshops, walk past offices for design, architecture and urban planning, as well as those of software companies, discover a gym, and finally get supervision to cultivate organic vegetables in small beds in a roof garden. But what is the connection between all of this?

In Japan, when a job is finished and the results are celebrated, or at the end of the year in a company, or after a traditional festival, a ritual is held. Everyone claps hands, not anyway they please but together: three claps in quick succession, which is repeated for a total of three times. This is followed by one final clap of release. In numbers: 3-3-3-1.

This is the philosophy of it all: just as, in a school, everyone learns something new, but in each classroom something different is learned, here at 3331 everyone produces something new and creative, and joyfully presents the results when the work is done.

That is why the school-like character of the building was kept. In the lobby you see old blackboards. In the plain corridors you pass the large old communal washbasins, and markings on the floor in various colours show the way, as it used to be. And so you pass through what were once classrooms, marvelling like a schoolchild, and realise that you will experience something new the next time you come.

Address アーツ千代田 3331, 3331 Arts Chiyoda, Sotokanda 6-11-14, Chiyoda-ku, 101–0021 Tokyo, www.3331.jp/en | **Getting there** Ginza metro line to Suehirocho, 3-minute walk | **Hours** Depending on exhibition or event | **Tip** For a contrast to contemporary design and art, walk approx. 10 minutes in the direction of Ueno Park to the Shitamachi Museum. Here life-size models depict the life of working people in the Edo period.

2 _ The 3-D Trick Art Museum

Become part of a work of art

Be as acrobatic as a ninja or as bold as a torero facing up to a raging bull. Take a trip back in time into Japanese history, get frightened out of your wits by monsters in a haunted house or by a skeleton that strokes your head. All of this is possible in the 3-D Trick Art Museum.

Because this museum works according to its own rules. You are not merely allowed to take photographs of the works of art and touch them – you can even walk on them in your shoes. The focus is on enjoyment. The museum exhibits 3-D images based on the principle of optical illusion. The technique known as trompe l'oeil conjures spatial depth that does not truly exist on a flat surface. If three-dimensional things such as people are part of the motif, the effect is particularly striking on a photo. And if your facial expression on the photo is dramatic enough, people who are not initiated into the secret will be amazed and have no doubt that you were balancing on a narrow beam above a deep abyss, even though there was nothing dangerous at all about the way the photograph was taken. The more talent as an actor you demonstrate, the more fun you will have later when looking at the images.

In 1987 Kazumune Kenju, the best-known exponent of trick art in Japan, founded the first creative studio for this genre. In 1991 the first 3-D trick art museum was then opened. Since then, this entertaining form of art has become well known internationally. Many exhibitions were held in the USA, as well as in Hong Kong, Singapore, Taiwan and South Korea.

In Tokyo there are two trick art museums. One of them is located in Hachioji, the other in Odaiba. Here we recommend the latter, because, in addition to a 'best of' collection from across the country, there is also an exhibition of motifs of old Japan. Famous works of art from the Edo period were taken as the models for the images.

Address 東京トリックアート迷宮館, Tokyo Trick Art Museum, Decks Tokyo Beach Island Mall 4F, Daiba 1-6-1, Minato-ku, 135−0091 Tokyo, www.trickart.info | **Getting there** Yurikamome Line to Odaiba-Kaihinkoen, 2-minutes walk, and Rinkai Line to Tokyo-Teleport, 5-minute walk | **Hours** Daily 11am−9pm | **Tip** On the fourth floor of the building next door is the Takoyaki Museum. It is not a classic museum but a collection of small restaurants that serve a speciality from Osaka: octopus balls in spicy sauce.

3__ The Aid Organisation
Committed to a good cause

It will be years before reconstruction has been completed in the coastal regions of east Japan that were devastated by the tsunami. For this reason there is still a need for volunteers to support local people who suffered from the damage. Tono Magokoro Net is one of the organisations that runs aid projects. This group was founded in the town of Tono in Iwate, and its sphere of action has now expanded far beyond the boundaries of Tono.

Anyone who is interested in helping can get information from the office in Tokyo. Volunteers who can translate Japanese texts into foreign languages are in demand, and donations are gratefully accepted.

In the current projects in the affected regions, the focus is on support for local authorities' efforts at reconstruction. It is important to give impulses to the economy, which means that agriculture is one of the main areas of activity. Every helping hand is urgently needed to make fields that were completely wrecked by the tsunami fertile again. Support is required at, for example, removing weeds from the wheat – a laborious and back-breaking task, as helpers have to bend over to pick out the weeds while making sure that they do not trample down the wheat. A further area of operation is in assisting in facilities for people with disabilities and senior citizens, taking the strain off the employees there. In order to bring a little joy to the population of the crisis-hit regions, a special campaign was called into being in the year when the catastrophe happened: every December, 100 Father Christmases are sent to eastern Japan to distribute sweets to victims of the disaster.

Whatever kind of work you do as a volunteer, the organisation appreciates it if there is enough time left at the end of the day to speak to the affected people about what happened to them. This experience enhances the lives of the helpers.

Address 遠野真心ネット, Tono Magokoro Net 3F, Kanda Higashi-Matsushita-cho 19, Chiyoda-ku, 101–0042 Tokyo, +81 (0) 362 064 697, www.tonomagokoro.net/english | Getting there Shinjuku metro line to Iwamoto-cho, 4-minute walk | Hours Mon–Fri 10am–6pm | Tip In the Yanagi-Mori-Jinja Shrine, the raccoon (tanuki) is venerated. If you replace the character for tanuki by two others that are pronounced in the same way, the meaning is 'to overtake others' or 'to get a lead'. The Japanese love a play on words like this.

4— The Aluminium Sculpture
An artist's view of the city

Since 2006 the park of the Tokyo Midtown lifestyle centre in Roppongi has been the site of a monumental aluminium sculpture that is an object of amazement and a photo motif for the people of Tokyo and tourists alike. Although *Caverna Lunaris* has long had the status of a landmark, hardly anyone knows about the creative person who was responsible for it.

His name is Florian Claar, a German who went to Japan in 1994 to turn his artistic visions into reality. He studied art in Stuttgart, specialising in installations and sculpture. Even in his early years, the connections between art, stage performance, architecture and music were important to him, and to this day they remain an indispensable part of his projects.

This versatile artist now has an international reputation: his sculptures and art-for-architecture works enrich public spaces not only in Japanese cities but are also in great demand in China and Taiwan.

Even after living here for 20 years, Tokyo still provides inspiration for the artist: 'I regard the city as a wilderness, as a wild garden, where people and architecture form an organic entity that is in a state of permanent change. The appearance of the city alters so quickly that a district that you have not visited for a while is unrecognisable after a few years and can be rediscovered as if it were new.' Claar is fascinated not only by the city, but also by the tolerance of Japanese society, which is always open to technical innovations and to new media, and above all by the Japanese audience for art, which took enthusiastically to media art at a very early stage.

His recommendation to visitors to the *Caverna Lunaris* work is that they should not only view the sculpture from a distance, but should also come closer in order to look through its openings, as the beholder's perception of it changes according to the distance.

Address Tokyo Midtown, Akasaka 9-7-1, Minato-ku, 107–0052 Tokyo, www.florianclaar.com | Getting there Oedo and other metro lines to Roppongi | Tip In the Tokyo Midtown shopping centre, the Suntory Museum of Art puts on attractive exhibitions.

5__Arakawa Amusement Park
A fair from bygone days

Where do you find hyper-modern amusement parks? In Japan. They have the fastest and craziest rides. There are two Disney parks and one Hello Kitty. It's hard to imagine that there was a time when people went to parks for the fairground atmosphere rather than their superlatives. If you like to wallow in nostalgia from time to time and yearn for the fairs of your childhood, then this is the one for you.

Arakawa-Yuen was the very first amusement park in the Japanese capital. To reach it, take the Toden Line, one of the two remaining tram routes in Tokyo. The ride there at a leisurely pace will put you in the right mood for your trip down memory lane. When the Toden trams went into operation in 1911, the Shinkansen was no more than a vision for the future. The Toden trams run in the north of the city, on a network that is twelve kilometres long.

The Arakawa Amusement Park was built in the 1950s to give space for play to the children and young people of a population that was growing rapidly at that time. The entrance prices were extremely low, and have remained so to this day: adults pay 200 yen for admission, children and senior citizens 100 yen. The price of a ticket for the rides is also 100 yen. Usually the numbers of visitors are modest, which means that you do not have to stand patiently in queues for a long time.

Hardly anything seems to have changed on the Arakawa-Yuen grounds since the park was first founded. Even the rides, most of them small and not particularly fast, are survivals from an age when people still used that old-fashioned word 'carousel'. In addition to these rides there is a children's zoo with small animals and an area for angling. It is possible that older kids will feel a little bit bored here, but the younger ones and adults with a tendency to nostalgia will definitely enjoy this trip back to the last century.

Address あらかわ遊園, Arakawa Amusement Park, Nishiogu 6-35-11, Arakawa-ku, 116–0011 Tokyo, +81 (0) 3 380 231 11, www.city.arakawa.tokyo.jp/yuuen (Japanese) | **Getting there** Toden Line to Arakawa-Yuenchi-mae | **Hours** Wed–Mon 9am–5pm, different hours on public holidays and during school holidays | **Tip** Five stops further on the Toden Line, Asukayama Park is especially worth a visit when the cherry trees are in flower.

6_Art Center Ongoing
Let's hope it carries on

The Art Center Ongoing in Kichijoji, a small and high-class art institution, lies outside the conservative and traditional gallery scene in Ginza, not only geographically but also in terms of its programme. The main point of difference to the usual galleries in Tokyo is that artists do not have to pay for their exhibitions here, as they usually do in Japan, but are chosen, and then have the opportunity to present their works at Ongoing. Thus the gallery is not focussed on established or well-to-do artists but provides an artistic home for the young and the avant-garde.

The institution emerged from a project at the start of the century, when a group of the 'young and wild' met once a year to discuss their work and to conceive an exhibition for it. As this was an ongoing project that had no fixed end, the name for the programme was born – and is always written in English, even in Japanese texts issued by the group.

What started out as an annual event finally took on a permanent form in 2008 at the Art Center Ongoing, with a fixed location for holding discussions and putting on exhibitions for one generation after the other. In this way, young artists have a home for their works, which are sometimes bulky, and always both unconventional and exciting. Furthermore, the Art Center Ongoing organises a three-month artist-in-residence programme, which includes accommodation and an exhibition.

When you step inside the gallery, it is easy to get your bearings in the rooms. The staircase on the right leads up to the exhibition of the moment. If you head left instead, you find yourself in the café – or, later in the day, in the bar – where opening nights and discussion evenings take place. Here you can linger over a drink or eat a snack, browse through an art book from the library, or purchase an avant-garde work of art from the shop.

Address Art Center Ongoing, Kichijoji Higashi-cho 1-8-7, Musashino-shi, 180–0002 Tokyo, www.ongoing.jp/en | **Getting there** JR-Chuo or Keio-Inokashira Line to Kichijoji, 10-minute walk | **Hours** Wed–Sun noon–11pm (gallery until 9pm) | **Tip** On the way to or from Kichijoji station you can go shopping on Sun Road, where the Linde bakery produces original German bread.

7__ The Bamba Hotel

Accommodation exclusively reserved for you

International hotel chains provide immaculate service. Everything is perfectly organised, so that guests never have to wait long for anything, even when the hotel is fully booked. However, such well-oiled guest-processing machinery does not always give stressed holidaymakers a relaxing experience. For travellers who attach less importance to luxury but appreciate a hotel stay in a family atmosphere, Takashi Watanabe has thought out a special VIP concept.

The Bamba Hotel is situated in Shinagawa. Opened in 2014, it is named after the area, the meaning of the word being 'place of horses': in the Edo period, the last post station in Edo on the route to Kyoto stood on this site. Watanabe purchased a 70-year-old building and saved it from demolition. With the help of local people, he restored it from top to bottom. The rooms were furnished with great attention to detail. Watanabe succeeded in preserving the charm of the old house, creating a mix of interiors that are fundamentally Japanese with the addition of a few pieces of Western-style furniture. This has produced cosy surroundings where the intention is that every guest should feel at home. No two rooms are alike, which arouses in visitors a curiosity to explore every corner of the building.

The Bamba Hotel is operated according to the one-group principle: during their stay, the house is reserved exclusively for a guest and his or her companions. People travelling alone can also book a room, of course. The hotel service does not cease when you leave the premises: on request, a guide will accompany you and show you around the Shinagawa district free of charge. Guests from abroad are given mobile phones so that they can be 'rescued' round the clock should they happen to get lost. There is always somebody at hand, to help no matter what the problem may be. With all of this service, you will feel like a VIP.

Address Bamba Hotel, Minami-Shinagawa 1-1-2, Shinagawa-ku, 140–004 Tokyo, +81 (0) 3 671 294 40, www.47gawa.tokyo/bamba/en | **Getting there** Keikyu Line (local) to Shin-Bamba | **Tip** The owner of Halleluya-Kobo (Halleluya Studio), a DIY store where workshops on restoring craftworks, furniture and antiques are held, had a leading role in renovating the Bamba Hotel. Mr Watanabe will be pleased to show you the way.

8__ The Bamboo Boutique
Once at the forefront – today a follower of fashion

Many fashion trends originated in the streets of Harajuku. This was the case in the early 1980s, when a completely new look appeared. Young people wore imaginative outfits that they bought in the boutique named Takenoko (bamboo shoot). After the shop that initiated this style of fashion they were known as takenoko-zoku (the tribe of bamboo children).

In 1978 the owner, Takenori Otake, established his boutique in Takeshita-Dori. As the character for bamboo occurred in both his first name and his family name, and the boutique was situated in the 'street beneath the bamboo', the name of the shop was an obvious choice. It sold fashion that differed sharply from the style of the time. The materials were shiny and seemed cheap. The colours were gaudy, with luminous shades of red, pink and purple to the fore. It was a wild stylistic mixture of the Arabian Nights and kimono. The clothes were worn loosely on the body. The 'bamboo style' would never have been accepted in the world of established fashion.

From the late 1970s a section of road in Harajuku was closed to motorised traffic on Sundays and put at the disposal of young people. The bamboo children met there to sing and dance to the sounds of disco music. At its peak it attracted up to 2,000 young people, and many onlookers. Following the attack carried out in Tokyo in 1995 by the Aum sect, this Sunday happening was judged by the authorities to be a safety risk. The offical status of a pedestrian zone was therefore reversed step by step up to 1998, and the young lost the space where they could be themselves. This sealed the end of the bamboo children. Years earlier, their look had already been overtaken by newer fashion trends.

Today Takenoko no longer sets the style for young people, but follows trends on the street. For almost 40 years this store has braved the buffeting of time, like a bamboo in the wind.

Address ブッティック・竹の子, Boutique Takenoko, Jingu-mae 1-6-15, Shibuya-ku, 150–0001 Tokyo | **Getting there** JR-Yamanote Line to Harajuku, 5-minute walk | **Hours** Daily 11am–8pm | **Tip** 5-minute walk from the boutique, in the Ota Ukiyoe Museum, you will find well-known Japanese prints.

9 ___ The Bargain Shop
Furniture made in jail

This address is a little-known tip for bargain hunters and a treasure trove for craftwork and furniture in traditional style. How about a cast-iron tea kettle for 1,400 yen or a handmade chest of drawers of solid wood with metal fittings for 26,000 yen? These items are not only suspiciously cheap, but also often of wickedly good quality.

Do you think there must be a catch? Well yes, they are products made by Japanese prisoners and sold by the Correctional Association Prison Industry Cooperation, CAPIC for short. Through the proceeds of sale in the shop, the prison inmates can save money to help them through the time after their release. Part of the profits is donated to social projects, for example to give support to victims of crime.

The range of products sold under the prison label goes far beyond the field of arts and crafts. If you are setting up house for the first time or would like to keep the cost of acquisitions low because your budget is limited or you are living in Japan only for a limited period, you can find most of what you need at CAPIC. The porcelain cups, with a price tag of 70 yen, are even cheaper than those in the numerous 100-yen stores. You will also find grocery items here, a big assortment of traditional wooden toys, soap, leather products, and much, much more. Among the most popular items are bags and aprons in the Marugoku series, which are made by inmates of the prison in Hakodate (Hokkaido). The lettering 'Prison' is printed, quite unmistakably, on the hard-wearing fabric. Soap of the Blue Stick brand is suitable for removing even the most stubborn stains.

Simply click your way through the product range: every item is available for sale online. Alternatively you can go to one of the branches of CAPIC in Fuchu, Nakano or Yokohama and examine the assortment and the quality of the articles for yourself.

Address CAPIC, Harumi-cho 4-10, Fuchu-shi, 183–0057 Tokyo, www.e-capic.com (Japanese) | Getting there JR-Musashino Line to Kita-Fuchu, 5-minute walk | Hours Mon–Fri 10am–4pm | Tip Okunitama-Jinja is one stop by train or a 30-minute walk from the prison shop. On the site of this extremely important shrine are a sumo ring and a Russo-Japanese war memorial.

10__Bobotei

Off to base camp

Far away in the northeast of Tokyo, in a remote dead-end street, is a special tavern. From the front garden with its barbecue area you have a view through sliding doors of the interior of a wooden building that consists of only one large room. On the right is a bar counter with a tiny kitchen, on the left set into the floor an irori, now a rare sight: a traditional hearth that warms guests from the end of October to March. When you have taken off your shoes and entered, you will immediately be greeted warmly by the landlord, Satoru Mishima.

Mishima was an editor in a publishing house for 30 years, but gave up this employment because of his love of books: he had lost interest in publishing purely commercial works with a short shelf life. Since then he has continued to be a freelance editor of books, now of long sellers on subjects that are close to his heart, for example environmental and social issues. Through his work at the publishing house and decades of work as an environmentalist, he has built up an extensive network of authors and photographers, ranging from one of the icons of the American hippie movement, Gary Snyder, to local persons who share Mishima's ideals of a better, more attractive society.

This explains why he runs a tavern. After leaving the publisher he opened an establishment in Higashimurayama that served as a curry restaurant by day and a bar by night. Now 67 years old, he wanted to slow down a little, so he closed the large restaurant-bar in order to open Bobotei two days a week right next to his home. But he has never regarded these enterprises merely as a source of income. Mishima calls them a little 'base camp' for a peaceful and friendly community. Therefore he introduces his guests to one another, and in no time at all, stimulating conversations are struck up over a delicious bite to eat and some good sake.

Address 茫々亭, Bobotei, Noguchicho 3-11-8, Higashimurayama-shi, 189–0022 Tokyo, +81 (0) 42 391 2365 | **Getting there** Seibu bus no. 35 to Megurita, 2-minute walk | **Hours** Fri & Sat 6–11pm; it is a good idea to phone in advance, as the times can vary | **Tip** Close by is Issui, a low-cost Chinese restaurant that serves tasty menus with generous portions. A recommendation is kuroyakisoba, a noodle dish with a spicy black sauce. Here you can also practise angling in a fishpond.

11__The Book Hotel

Accommodation with a bedtime book

What gives more pleasure than reading a good book? What could be better than immersing yourself in a story and not putting the book down until you have read the very last page? And where, except within your own four walls, do you have the opportunity today to leaf through a book without any inhibitions? Such a place, where lovers of reading can devote themselves undisturbed to their pastime, was created in 2015, when the Book and Bed Hotel opened in Ikebukuro.

The idea behind this guesthouse is described as 'an overnight stay in a bookshop'. However, you can't buy the books. The phrase was coined simply to describe the atmosphere. On the long wall of shelves that rise from the floor to the ceiling there is space for up to 3,000 books and mangas. This assortment of literature includes reading matter in various languages, and the collection is growing constantly. Guests can settle down comfortably with their book on a broad settee, or talk with their friends there, or strike up a conversation with other guests.

There is no official bedtime at the Book and Bed. When your eyelids start to droop, you simply withdraw into your sleeping capsule, which is behind the wall of books, or to the dormitory. A 24-hour supermarket in the same building and a neighbourhood bakery, which sells fresh rolls until two o'clock in the morning, ensure that you don't go hungry late at night.

But don't expect to be spoiled at the Book and Bed. You will find neither single rooms with their own bathroom nor luxurious beds. To compensate, guests enjoy the ultimate reading experience. The price of an overnight stay is no higher than in a youth hostel, and free WiFi is part of the service. Guests who don't want a bed for the night but would like to stay in the reading room for a while or rest in the dormitory are also welcome to do this for a modest charge.

Address Book and Bed Tokyo, 7F, Nishi-Ikebukuro 1-17-7, Toshima-ku, 171–0021 Tokyo, +81 (0) 3 642 175 95, www.bookandbedtokyo.com | Getting there JR-Yamanote Line and others to Ikebukuro, west exit | Tip Foreigners in Japan often complain that the bread is soft and boring, but you will find a wide range of tasty loaves at the Mitsuwa bakery in Ikebukuro Station.

12__ The Bridge Over the Kanda

Crossing the ages

The Kanda river, almost 25 kilometres long, is one of Tokyo's main rivers, even though it seems small in comparison to the Sumida and Arakawa. Its source is far in the west, at the Inokashira pond in Kichijoji, and it originally flowed into Tokyo Bay in the district that is now called Hibiya. As Edo needed fresh water when it became a seat of government in around 1600, some of its water was diverted to Koishikawa, while the rest of the river was channelled along the outer wall of Edo's castle as a moat, and then north to the Sumida. Enormous earthworks were necessary for this purpose, as the view from the Hijiri Bridge shows: the canyon through which the Kanda flows here was cut into the plain at that time.

The Hijiri Bridge itself, by contrast, was constructed much more recently, in 1927, after the big Kanto earthquake. It was built of reinforced concrete, an extremely modern technology in those days. The name means 'holy bridge', as it connects two religious places: the Russian Orthodox Cathedral of Saint Nikolai on the south bank of the Kanda, and the Confucian Yushima-Seido Temple to the north of the river. From the bridge you also have a view of Ochanomizu Station, which went into operation in 1904, as well as the metro line, which has been running since 1954 and crosses the water here.

Thus this crossing is a meeting place at which transport routes dating from different centuries come together: the waterways, which carried a lot of traffic in the Edo period, were replaced in the early twentieth century by railways as the principal means of transport, which in turn was complemented by road traffic in the second half of the century. When you stand here, don't just enjoy the prospect to the east. If you go to the Shohei Bridge opposite, you will have a wonderful view of the Hijiribashi, especially if you go there as the sun sets.

Address 聖橋, Hijiri Bridge, Kanda Surugadai 4, Chiyoda-ku, 101–0062 Tokyo | **Getting there** JR-Chuo Line and others to Ochanomizu | **Tip** You can visit the Cathedral of Saint Nikolai and the Yushima-Seido Temple, which gave the bridge its name, or walk past the Shitamachi (Lower Town) along the Kanda to its mouth.

13__ The Concept Store
Recommended by shopping experts

A virtually infinite range of lifestyle products is available in Japan. Some innovations are practical and useful, while others seem to be completely superfluous for a normal way of life. But how do you find out which of them are an enhancement to everyday life, and which are not?

For customers who are feeling disoriented, a new kind of department store has opened in Futako-Tamagawa. Tsutaya-Kaden sells items connected with electronics, furniture, clothing, the household, food, health and beauty, music, and travel. The store's special feature is that goods are not arranged by price or manufacturer but according to their purpose – this means according to the lifestyle that they match. Books and magazines are also on sale here, as the concept store is based in a branch of the Tsutaya bookshop chain.

The moment customers enter the store, they are given the impression that they are staying in a luxury hotel. Sales staff – they are actually known as concierges – await at the reception and it is immediately clear that they have time for you and are pleased to help with your shopping. It really works like this: you tell the concierge something about yourself, and on the basis of the information that you supply, an individually tailored package of articles is selected. The offerings are not restricted to items such as electronic products and furniture, on which the store earns the highest margins, but relates to the entire product range. The aim is to ascertain your own personal requirements.

Your shopping consultant will also propose reading matter that matches your interests. You can then leaf through the chosen items at your leisure in the bookshop café. And it goes without saying that you can browse around the sales displays on your own. Everything should be just as you wish, because at Tsutaya-Kaden the customer is king.

Address 蔦屋家電, Tsutaya-Electrics, Futako-Tamagawa-Rise, Tamagawa 1-14-1, Setagaya-ku, 158–0094 Tokyo | **Getting there** Tokyu-Oimachi Line to Futako-Tamagawa | **Hours** Daily 9.30am–10.30pm | **Tip** The Seikado Museum is reached in eight minutes by minibus from Futako-Tamagawa station. Here you will find an art collection and rare literary items from more than ten centuries, especially works from China.

14__ The Cosplay Convention
A costume festival for young people

Cosplay comes from Japan, and nowhere else is it practised so excessively. It is a form of youth culture that has a big fan base in other countries, so visiting a cosplay event is right at the top of the agenda for many tourists in Japan. The best-known of these events is the costume spectacle on the fringe of Komike, the world's biggest comics fair. However, Komike only takes place twice a year – so where else can you encounter the double of Miku Hatsune or Pikachu?

Two places where cosplay conventions are regularly held are Tokyo Leisure Land in Odaiba and the Toshimaen amusement park in Nerima. In the former, it is possible to attend an event almost every weekend. The admission price is 2,000 yen, regardless of whether you are in costume or have just come as a spectator. Even outside the event zone there are opportunities to see costumed young people taking selfies on the big wheel or with some other attractive backdrop; it is worth visiting the convention just to see the cosplay photographers, who are known as 'camera kozo', at work.

In Tokyo Leisure Land you are allowed to use tripods, reflectors and other aids to photography. That is why it is the recommended option for professional photographers. However, a few rules were introduced that have to be respected, because in the past there were some incidents with people who were too pushy when taking their snapshots. Please do not press the shutter button until the models have taken up their poses. Those who want motifs that go beyond the usual posing should ask for permission beforehand. If you ask politely, invisible doors are opened. The cosplayers are pleased when you show interest in what they are doing. And before you know it, you are in conversation with a perfect copy of your idol, and you can find out everything you always wanted to know about this youth cult of Japanese origin.

Address 東京レジャーランド, Tokyo Leisure Land, Palette-Town, Aomi 1-3-8, Koto-ku, 135–0064 Tokyo | **Getting there** Rinkai Line and others to Tokyo-Teleport, 5-minute walk | **Hours** Daily 11am–11pm (cosplay 10am–8pm) | **Tip** The Venus-Fort shopping centre is worth a visit for its beautiful ceiling paintings and constantly changing lighting and atmosphere, which create the impression that the times of day have been speeded up.

15__The Curry Station

A restaurant for railway nostalgia

Mr Ishida is a 'testudo-otaku', a dyed-in-the-wool train freak. He started collecting as a child: train tickets, station signs, passengers' hanging-straps, and so on and so forth. As his apartment was soon full to bursting point, and he wanted to share his passion with others, in 1963 he opened Japan's first railway restaurant and called it the Niagara Curry Station.

You can't miss this place, because even outside the restaurant, everything has the appearance of a station. A stop signal, a station clock and the cut-off front end of a steam locomotive in the window give visitors an advance impression of what awaits them inside. Before you are shown to your table, you get a 'ticket' for your order from a ticket machine. To help you make up your mind, a glass case is filled with the dishes that are on offer in the shape of plastic models. On request, an English-language menu is provided. Meatballs, escalopes and croquettes are on offer as side orders to go with the curry. For people who like their food to be spicy, there is the cho-tokkyu version, i.e. the super-express. Everything that the kitchen produces tastes delicious, and is good value for money.

The conductor – sorry, we mean the waiter, of course – will punch your ticket and take you to a seat. The restaurant is full of little surprises. While you are still admiring all of the owner's rail memorabilia and scanning every corner of the small room, a model train comes rattling to your table and delivers the dishes that you have ordered. The drinks are served by a young waitress wearing a Japanese railway employee uniform.

After running the restaurant for 50 years, Mr Ishida decided it was time to retire. However, he did not want to close down the Niagara Station, so he appointed his son to the position of stationmaster, and his daughter-in-law was promoted to manager of the dining car.

Address カレーステーションナイアガラ, Niagara-Curry, Yutenji 1-21-2, Meguro-ku,
153–0052 Tokyo, +81 (0)3 371 326 02, www.niagara-curry.com | **Getting there** Tokyu-
Toyoko Line (local) to Yutenji, 4-minute walk | **Hours** Tue, Wed, Fri–Sun 11am–8pm* |
Tip The Meguro-gawa (Meguro river) is a 20-minute walk away. Here you will see a few
chic boutiques, a bonsai shop and some nice cafés.

16___Daiba Park

From a defence facility to a leisure area

Today the man-made island of Odaiba in Tokyo Bay is a trendy place where people come to spend their leisure time. It is popular with both the Japanese and tourists from abroad. However, few of them are aware of the history of the island.

When the black American ships of Commodore Matthew Perry arrived at the city of Uraga in 1853, the shogunate of Tokugawa decided to protect the coast of Shinagawa by building eleven daiba (artillery batteries). The shogunate, which had hermetically sealed off Japan from the outside world for 250 years, was not prepared for the invasion. It possessed no large ships that could have defended the country in the event of an attack by a foreign power. Construction of the artillery emplacements was started in the same year, but only five of the eleven planned installations were ever completed. One reason was that the new treaty of friendship with the USA meant that the work was no longer urgently necessary. A further reason was simply lack of money. And in fact the completed batteries never fired a shot.

Today only the third and the sixth artillery emplacement still exist in their original condition. The government in Tokyo awarded them the status of historic monuments. The others were demolished to make way for the harbour that was opened in 1941. The third battery had to be restored following damage during the great Kanto earthquake of 1923. It is situated in Daiba Park, which opened in 1928. The sixth artillery emplacement stands on a nature island, which is no longer connected to the main island, and access to it is prohibited. That is why rare species of plants can be found there again, as well as wild birds that are at risk of extinction. If you stand on the Rainbow Bridge, which can be crossed on foot, or on the waterfront of the Daiba Park, you will be treated to a wonderful view of the island.

Address 台場公園, Daiba-Park, Daiba 1-10, Minato-ku, 135–0091 Tokyo | Getting there Yurikamome Line to Odaiba-Kaihinkoen, 12-minute walk | Tip Miraikan (The National Museum of Emerging Science and Innovation) gives you insights into tomorrow's world. To get there, go two stops on the Yurikamome Line to Fune-no-Kagakukan, from where the museum is five minutes' walk.

17_The Designer Teahouse
Teatime in the bamboo woods

A trip to the kabuki theatre is well worthwhile, not only for the performance on the stage. You can also look forward to a special visual and culinary experience at Jugetsudo, a teahouse and a shop specialising in nori, dried seaweed.

The internationally renowned architect Kengo Kuma was responsible for the interior. In the shop belonging to the kabuki theatre he used 3,000 bamboo poles to create an environment that is both modern and linked to Japanese culture. The room was completely clad with bamboo, giving visitors the impression that they are in the middle of a bamboo grove.

Kengo Kuma made his name above all with an inflatable teahouse in the shape of two joined-up footballs that was presented in 2007 in Frankfurt. At present he is engaged in planning a stadium for the next Olympic Games in Tokyo.

Jugetsudo is a company with a long tradition. Before it entered the tea business in 1980, its main field of activity was producing nori. Founded in 1854 in Tokyo, the enterprise was originally called Kawaguchi-ya, and later changed its name to Maruyama-Nori. Tea products are sold under the Jugetsudo brand name. The company was dedicated to excellent quality from the very beginning. In contrast to Kyoto, the former imperial city, the gourmet scene in Kanto was not highly developed in the nineteenth century. The company was therefore honoured when it was allowed to supply its marine products to the centre of culinary refinement, and even demanding noble clients appreciated the quality that was provided.

Green tea is preferably enjoyed with wagashi, a traditional sweetmeat made from rice flour and bean paste. In a tea tasting, held every morning from 11am to noon, you can find out which delicacies go best with which kind of tea. Reservation is recommended. From 7pm an evening menu with sandwiches, sushi and other snacks is served.

Address 寿月堂, Jugetsudo, Kabukiza-Tower 5F, Ginza 4-12-15, Chuo-ku, 104–0061 Tokyo, +81 (0) 3 627 876 26, www.maruyamanori.com | Getting there Hibiya Line to Higashi-Ginza, exit 3 | Hours Shop: daily 10am–7pm; teahouse & restaurant: daily 10am–11pm | Tip In Ginza there are exclusive Western cafés. One of them is known for its high-class interior: Ladurée Boutique Ginza.

18__ The District That Vanished

Out of map, out of mind?

In the north of Tokyo there is a district with a dark past. For a long time it was associated with poverty, crime and death. In 1966 the government removed Sanya from the street plan. What had happened?

In the early Edo period a ghetto for the burakumin, the lowest caste, was installed here. This caste was tasked with carrying out 'unclean' work – duties linked to blood such as slaughtering animals and processing animal products – for the shogunate, as Buddhist beliefs forbade the feudal ruling class to do this. The buraku were also responsible for executing criminals. 200,000 people were executed and buried in mass graves in Sanya over a period of 300 years.

Yoshiwara, a well-known quarter of brothels, was also situated in this district. After the Second World War, day labourers, the homeless, alcoholics and criminals gravitated to Sanya. They have now been joined by low-budget travellers from Japan and abroad who stay in accommodation that used to be reserved for Japanese workers.

Even today, 50 years after Sanya disappeared from the street map, the population structure of this worldly district has changed little. In 1966, its name was replaced by a different appellation, and furthermore it was also split up between the districts of Kiyokawa, Nihon-Tsutsumi and Higashi-Asakusa. Close to Minami-Senju station, a statue of Buddha is visible from the train. This is the site of the mass grave for people who were executed. In the neighbourhood of the station, at the border between the districts of Taito and Arakawa, there is a crossroads named Namida-Bashi (Bridge of Tears). The executions took place on this spot. The bridge no longer exists. It was possible to delete the name of Sanya, but the memories linger on.

Address 泪橋交差点, Namida-Bashi-Crossing, Minami-Senju 2-28, Arakawa-ku, 116–003 Tokyo, formerly Sanya in the district around 111–0022 Tokyo | **Getting there** Hibiya metro line to Minami-Senju | **Tip** Dote-no-Iseya, a traditional restaurant in Asakusa, has a stunning interior and the reputation of frying some of the best tempura in Tokyo.

19 _ The Dog Memorial
A late happy end for Hachiko

The story of Japan's most faithful dog is known across the globe. Thanks to the Hollywood blockbuster Hachiko (2009), which starred Richard Gere in the leading role, the whole world heard about the tragic fate of an Akita dog. While Hachiko was still alive, a bronze statue was erected in front of the Shibuya train station to honour his loyalty.

More recently, a second monument to the famous pet has been created. It was unveiled on 8 March, 2015 on the occasion of the 80th anniversary of his death. Also made of bronze, this 1.90-metre-high statue stands on the campus of the legendary Tokyo University in Bunkyo. The dog's owner, Hidesaburo Ueno, once worked there. He was a professor – not of music, like his well-known movie double, but of agriculture. The memorial was made on the initiative of his faculty and paid for entirely by donations. Although it is publicly accessible, crowds of sightseers have not turned up so far.

The bronze sculpture shows the dog delightedly greeting his master. You can truly feel the canine euphoria when his owner comes to pick him up at the end of a long day's wait. Hachiko is depicted joyfully jumping up and being rewarded with a pat on the neck. It was this scene of welcome that moved filmgoers to tears. This was clearly the moment that the dog was longing for when one day, unexpectedly, Ueno no longer returned to the rendezvous. Hachiko was only one and a half years old when the professor passed away at his place of work in 1925. Although his human best friend never came back again, the dog stuck to the daily ritual until the end of his life. Finally, when he was eleven years old, he was discovered lifeless in the streets of Shibuya.

Thanks to the new statue, a work by the sculptor Tsutomu Ueda, Hachiko and his master have at last been reunited. And so the story has found a happy end after all.

Address 東大ハチ公, Todai-Hachiko, Yayoi 1-1-1, Bunkyo-ku, 113–8657 Tokyo |
Getting there Nanboku metro line to Todai-Eki-mae, 3-minute walk | Tip The former
residence of Maeda, ruler of the region, is on the campus. The Akamon (Red Gate) was
built in 1827 on the occasion of his wedding with the daughter of a shogun.

20_Donzoko

Down and out since 1951

90 per cent of Shinjuku was in ruins in 1945, and the black market blossomed here in the immediate post-war period in provisional wooden huts. By now most of them have disappeared, and tall buildings have put their stamp on the district. However, in the area of Shinjuku-sanchome to the east of the train station between Meiji-dori and Yasukuni-dori you can still find low-rise remains of the old Shinjuku of the 1950s and 1960s.

In 1951, in a wooden shack, three drama students opened the pub Donzoko, named after Gorki's play *The Lower Depths*, which was translated into Japanese as *Down and Out*. A free interpretation of the students' choice of name would be their motto, that if you are no good for anything else, you can always open a pub. They had a modern attitude, admitting women to the tavern, which was an innovation at that time, but their lack of experience meant that the pub almost went bankrupt after a year, as too many customers got away without paying. Donzoko survived this and a fire in 1954, after which the existing pub was built. In the following years it was a focal point for intellectuals and young rebels. The progressive atmosphere of those days has remained in the three low, cramped storeys, which were constructed using large beams from an old temple. When Donzoko's 50th anniversary was celebrated in 2001, a book was published so that prominent customers – the writer Yukio Mishima is the best-known of them – could record their impressions.

When you enter, take care first of all that you don't bang your head. When you are sitting on one of the little chairs, you will surely be surprised at some of the items on the menu: alongside Japanese dishes you will find pizza and piroshki. The menu is still in part a survival from the 1950s, when such meals were exotic in Japan and could only be ordered in expensive foreign restaurants.

Address どん底, Donzoko, Shinjuku 3-10-2, Shinjuku-ku, 160–0022 Tokyo, +81 (0) 3 335 477 49, www.donzoko.co.jp | Getting there Shinjuku Line and others to Shinjuku-sanchome | Hours Daily 5pm–12.30am | Tip If you speak Japanese, a visit to the Suehirotei Rakugo theatre, where traditional Japanese comedy is performed, is highly recommended.

21__The Dyers' Lanes

Bygone Tokyo

Until the 1950s, the dyeing trade flourished in Nakai, where more than 300 small factories operated close to the river Myoshoji. It was one of Japan's largest districts of dyers, comparable with those in Kyoto and Kanazawa. The appearance of this quarter was characterised by the dyers, who rinsed their coloured fabrics in the river.

Although Nakai lies only a few stops by rail from Shinjuku, nothing remains here of the hustle and bustle of the city. It is a dreamy little district where time seems to have stood still. Close to the river there are numerous little shops that sell arts and crafts made from traditional fabrics and other materials.

The manga artist Fujio Akatsuka (1935–2008) lived in Nakai and took inspiration from the atmosphere of his surroundings. One of his best-known characters is the buffoon Bakabon. In Akatsuka's comics we read stories that happened outside his front door: shops, restaurants and even people from Nakai appear there under their real names.

If you take a walk through the narrow shopping streets, you will come across banners or posters bearing amusing cartoons. They are works by this artist, who was an active member of the local community and liked to have a public presence.

To preserve the memory of the traditional activity of this district, the festival of the dyers' lanes, Some-no-Komichi, was established in 2011. On this occasion the Myoshoji is turned into the 'River Gallery' once a year: long rolls of coloured cloth, which are called tan-mono, are stretched above the river Myoshoji from the Jisai Bridge to the Taisho Bridge. This cloth, fluttering in the wind, is intended as a reminder of the carp banners that are hoisted on the occasion of Children's Day. There is also a varied programme of exhibitions, workshops and guided tours. The festival is held over three days, always on the last weekend in February.

Address 染めの小道, Some-no-Komichi, Naka-Ochiai 1, 2 and Kamiochiai 2, Shinjuku-ku, 161–0032 Tokyo, www.somenokomichi.com (only Japanese) | **Getting there** Seibu-Shinjuku Line (local) or Oedo metro line to Nakai | **Tip** Sunmerry's bakery next to the station on the Seibu Line has a wide assortment of bread rolls, some of which are really delicious.

22 The Electricity Substation
A reminder of the war

Many traces of the Second World War have now disappeared in Tokyo. One monument that remains as a reminder of this dark chapter in Japanese history is located in Minami Park in Higashi-Yamato, a place where people now meet for sports or to play games.

The electric transformer station of the Hitachi company, which operated from 1938 until 1993, supplied power for manufacturing aircraft engines for warplanes. In 1945, at the end of the war, it was itself attacked by aircraft.

The nearby factory was severely damaged, but the transformer station, which is housed in a rectangular concrete block, was largely unscathed apart from a few bullet holes, and functioned for many years after the attack.

After the substation was decommissioned in 1993, the Tokyo city authorities took over the site in order to restore the war-damaged building. The numerous signs of battle that scarred its outer walls were not, however, removed, as the intention was to present to future generations the sobering subject of war and to prevent the history of the site from being forgotten.

In 1995 this place of memorial was officially listed as a historic monument. Since then it has been administered by the local government of Higashi-Yamato. The building is normally closed, but its interior can be visited from time to time when events are held there. You can already form a first impression of it from the surrounding fence, by taking a look through the façade with its windows.

On the same site, some further remains from past times are connected with the transformer station, among them a propeller from a fighter plane and a lump of concrete, once part of a water tower that was also destroyed in the air raids. Some pieces of metal that were formerly used in the manufacturing process in the Hitachi works have been set in concrete in the ground.

Address 旧日立航空機立川工場変電所, Kyu-Hitachi-Kokuki-Tachikawa-Kojo-Hendenjo, Minami-Koen, Sakuragaoka 2, Higashi-Yamato-shi, 207–0022 Tokyo | Getting there Seibu-Haijima Line and Tama monorail to Tamagawajosui, 5-minute walk | Tip The Itoyokado department store lies very close to the park. Its food department has a fantastic assortment. The main and side dishes produced there are absolutely delicious.

23 The Elephant Studio
Art, fashion, music and more

Takahiro Komatsu is a name that stands for success. The gallery named Elephant Studio is just one of many projects that he has initiated. After completing his course of study in fashion design in the year 2000 in Kyoto, he founded his Wa-to-Wa fashion label and revolutionised the kimono. He took aesthetic details of this traditional garment and combined them with Western fashion trends. He created comfortable, easy-to-wear items for young people such as tops, trousers and aprons. In search of further inspiration he lived in the European fashion centres of London and Paris for a considerable time.

If Komatsu had remained in the fashion world, he would undoubtedly have taken his place alongside the best in the business. However, that was not enough for him, so he looked for a new field of activity in branding and creative public relations.

The Elephant Studio was a small gallery in Shibuya for a long time. In 2015 it reopened with new offerings and more space. The exhibition area was extended by the addition of two more storeys. The result is a 'concept space', which alongside exhibitions can accommodate fashion shows, concerts, workshops and many more events.

The programme includes the works of both unknown and well-established artists. In 2016 two extremely successful photographers, Katsuo Hanzawa and Takayuki Okada, were invited to show their work, and further renowned national and international artists are expected.

Since the reopening, a restaurant and a bar have been added to the gallery. Café and Macrobi serves healthy and delicious dishes taken from Japanese cuisine. For the restaurant it is important that the ingredients that end up on the customer's plate are produced in harmony with nature. In the bar, Tenjiku, you can also get tasty snacks as well as a selection of trendy cocktails. The Elephant Studio is about much more than the consumption of art.

Address エレファントスタジオ, Elephant Studio, Shibuya 2-7-4, Shibuya-ku, 150–0002 Tokyo, +81 (0) 80 471 706 11, www.elephant.tokyo | **Getting there** JR Yamanote Line and others to Shibuya, 10-minute walk | **Hours** Gallery: daily 11am–8pm | **Tip** A 15-minute walk away, close to the Aoyama-Dori-Omote-Sando crossing, the Nezu Museum houses the private collection of the industrialist Kaichiro Nezu (1860–1940) and displays more than 7,000 treasures of Asian and Japanese art.

24__The Face of Baymax
The source of inspiration for Disney

If you come to Tokyo as a tourist, you will probably visit the Hanazono Shrine in Shinjuku. It is a little bit out of the way, directly behind the shopping street, and is an oasis of tranquillity in this fast-moving quarter of the city. Here you can get away from the hustle and bustle for a little while and recharge your batteries for the next activity.

In 2011 the Hollywood director Don Hall was looking around the city in search of inspiration for a new Disney anime. He too paid a visit to this religious site and said in an interview: 'In a shrine in Tokyo I looked up and saw the bell. Then I felt relaxed, calm and peaceful.'

Among the five bells there, it was the huge shrine bell that inspired him to create the face of the hero Baymax in *Big Hero 6*. He changed the shape a little. The two circular openings that are connected by a long, narrow slit on the bottom of the bell were made into the facial features of the cute robot. One of his colleagues took care of the body: the result was a charming, roundly plump marshmallow robot that you want to hug straight away.

The blockbuster movie premiered in the cinemas in 2014, and was a big success at the box office. Following its nomination for an Oscar, a delegation – including a human-sized Baymax – visited the shrine. A ceremony was performed to give the team divine assistance, so that it would not return empty-handed from the awards event. Fortune did indeed smile on the movie team, as the film was voted the best anime of 2015 and won the Academy Award.

The secular representatives of the Hanazono Shrine were also delighted that their bell had provided the inspiration for a Disney anime. They expressed their thanks for the welcome favourable publicity by presenting a bell to Baymax. It was, of course, shaped just like the bell that was used as a model for his face.

Address 花園神社, Hanazono Shrine, Shinjuku 5-17-3, Shinjuku-ku, 160–0022 Tokyo | **Getting there** Marunouchi metro line and others to Shinjuku-sanchome, exit E 2 | **Tip** The Golden Gai next to the Hanazono Shrine is an old lane with a lot of tiny, atmospheric bars.

25__The Fans' Rendezvous

In the footsteps of Haruki Murakami

Haruki Murakami is one of the most popular contemporary authors. He often writes about locations that he has visited himself, and his most loyal fans follow his tracks everywhere. In Tokyo, too, there are places where his stories were set. Before you set off in search of them, it is worth paying a visit to Rokujigen, where fans of the writer from all over the world congregate.

In 2010 the travel journalist and TV director Kunio Nakamura took over an old jazz pub in Ogikubo. It was a run-down bar in an old house behind railway tracks, and he chose it deliberately. He changed nothing about the worn wooden interior of the tavern, except that instead of old jazz records, the shelves are now filled with rows of books. Nakamura has created a distinctive atmosphere in order to give guests the impression that they have come to a location from a novel by their favourite author.

The pub is not only a meeting place for followers of Murakami but also a literary café, where works by other authors are presented and discussed by the members of a reading circle. Nevertheless, in Rokujigen (The Sixth Dimension) the focus is on one specific famous Japanese author. Nakamura collects all the information he can get about his idol, as well as his works in every language he can find. In 2014 he published a travel guide that enables readers to easily track down the places mentioned in Murakami's books.

Nakamura is now consulted by Murakami fans from all over the world. From the press, too, he receives the strangest inquiries, and people often believe that he is the master's agent. Again and again he gets requests from people who hope to be put in contact with the author, but has to admit quietly that so far he has never had an opportunity to meet his role model Haruki Murakami. All the same, Rokujigen is the ideal starting point for a journey into Murakami's world.

Address 6次元, Rokujigen 2F, Kamiogi 1-10-3, Suginami-ku, 167–0043 Tokyo,
+81 (0) 3 339 335 39, rokujigen_ogikubo@yahoo.co.jp | Getting there JR-Chuo Line
(local) to Ogikubo, west exit, 3-minute walk | Hours Daily 3–10pm (sometimes the hours
are changed, so it is best to phone before going) | Tip 3-minute walk away is Ogikubo-
Hakusan-Jinja, a shrine that people visit because it is said to alleviate toothache.

26 The First Airport

Where Japan learned to fly

On the site in Tokorozawa that was once Japan's first airport, today there is a large park with an aviation museum in its grounds. On the way to the museum, visitors are greeted by the sight of two historic aircraft. At the exit to Kokukoen train station is an Air Nippon YS-11A dating from 1969, and close to the museum a Curtiss-Wright C-46, a cargo plane made in 1950. These exhibits give visitors a foretaste of what awaits them inside.

A look around the exhibition hall on the first floor is a treat for any fan of aviation. A large number of Japanese and American aircraft, and helicopters too, fill this large space. Visitors can enter several of the aircraft on the floor of the hall and gain a vague impression of what a sublime feeling it must have been to fly them. More exhibits are suspended from the ceiling. From the upper floor a walkway gives access to them.

According to the museum information, the first aircraft took off from the landing strip at Tokorozawa in 1911. It flew to a height of ten metres, stayed in the air for 1 minute and 20 seconds, and covered a distance of 800 metres. However, the exhibits are not only devoted to history. Interactive items give visitors an idea of what it is like to be an aviator. On the flight simulator they can practise taking off and landing. Another simulator demonstrates how the air-traffic controllers work in the airport tower. In the small museum cinema, a regularly changing selection of films on the subject of aviation is screened.

In 1945, following the end of the Second World War, the American armed forces took control of the airport at Tokorozawa. It was returned to Japan in the early 1980s. Soon afterwards, this historic site became the Aviation Museum and the Tokorozawa Aviation Memorial Park (Kokukoen), which has become a popular place for recreation.

Address 所沢航空公園と所沢航空発祥記念館, Tokorozawa Aviation Memorial Park and Tokorozawa Aviation Museum, Namiki 1-13, 359−0042 Tokorozawa | Getting there Seibu-Shinjuku Line (local) to Kokukoen, 8-minute walk | Hours Tue−Sun 9.30am−5pm (last admission 4.30pm)* | Tip At the Shin-Arai-cho crossroads you will find Kurakata-Ningyo, a specialist shop selling doll's shrines and showcases for the girls' festival and the boys' festival.

27__The Flyover

Overshadowed by mobility

Everywhere in Tokyo you come across highways raised on pillars. They enable cars to move across the city relatively fast. As in all Japanese metropolitan areas, lack of space makes it necessary to raise traffic above the ground in Tokyo. The elevated roads cut through the sea of buildings, pass over ground-level city streets in which traffic lights stop the flow of cars every few metres, or follow a sinuous path above the canals, which were the principal transport routes in Edo in past times.

Plans to construct these urban highways already existed before the Second World War, but their implementation only began after the war ended. An impetus for this was provided by the Olympic Games in Tokyo in 1964, when the authorities wished to avoid traffic gridlock.

To minimise the costs of buying land, the highways were built above normal roads and the canals that pass through much of the centre of Tokyo. The city's most famous bridge, Nihonbashi, fell victim to this development: now situated beneath a huge expressway, it has lost its old charm.

If you are travelling from Narita Airport to the city centre, take the airport bus above the buildings and between skyscrapers by 'flying' into Tokyo (from Haneda the urban highway to the inner city is mostly in tunnels). If you would like to feel the effect of the flyover roads from a frog's-eye view, look for places where they intersect, as from here they appear especially dominant and crushing.

One such intersection, which is also easy to reach with public transport, lies – or rather stands – in front of Sunshine 60, a skyscraper in Ikebukuro, where an approach road leads up to the elevated highway. After taking a look at the flyover from below, you can take a lift up to the observation deck of the high-rise. From the 60th floor, the great traffic arteries almost look cute.

Address Higashi-Ikebukuro 3-3-2, Toshima-ku, 170–0013 Tokyo | Getting there
JR-Yamanote Line and others to Ikebukuro, 10-minute walk | Tip The site of Sunshine 60
was once occupied by Sugamo prison. Until the end of the war it was a jail for political
prisoners, later for war criminals. Today only a memorial stone with the inscription 'For Peace'
serves as a reminder of this.

28__Fukagawa-Fudo-do
The narrow path between ancient and modern

The temple of Fukagawa-Fudo-do in Monzen-Nakacho is distinguished by a high level of spirituality. This religious site belongs to the Buddhist Shingon sect, which was founded in 1703 and has its headquarters in the city of Narita in Chiba Prefecture.

The old and the new main temple halls of Fukagawa-Fudo-do, which are directly adjacent to each other, could hardly present a greater contrast. The old wooden structure dating from 1863 originally belonged to the Ryufukuji Temple in Chiba. Following the destruction in the Second World War of the old main hall in Monzen-Nakacho, a subsidiary foundation, it was not rebuilt, but replaced by an existing building that was moved to the location.

The new main hall was not completed until 2011. It was built to a modern design, with the entire façade of the cuboid building decorated with a pattern of Sanskrit characters in black and gold. Inside, a remarkable visual experience awaits visitors: 9,500 small statues of Buddha made from crystal glass flank the approach via a long corridor. Next to the old main hall stands a further new structure. It is home to the 'treasure chamber of the sun god', which is situated on the fourth floor. The name delivers on its promise: in a large space, an imposing statue of the sun god (Dainichi) has been placed. The ceiling was adorned with a gigantic Buddha and lotus flowers by the famous painter Chinami Nakajima. A group of golden Buddha figures surrounds the deity.

An installation on the first floor demonstrates the nature of the pilgrimage around the island of Shikoku, which follows in the footsteps of Kukai, the founder of the Shingon sect. Those who want to save the effort of this 1,200-kilometre journey, but without missing its spiritual benefits, have the opportunity to make a donation and to pray at this temple. This is said to have the same beneficial effect.

Address 深川不動堂, Fukugawa-Fudo-do, Tomioka 1-17-13, Koto-ku, 135–0047 Tokyo | **Getting there** Tozai metro line and others to Monzen-Nakacho, exit 1 | **Hours** Daily 9am–4pm (upper floor), 9am–5.45pm (ground floor) | **Tip** Extremely impressive daily ceremonies are held at Fukagawa-Fudo-do. At Fukagawa-Edo-Shiryokan, approximately one kilometre away, a typical city quarter from the first half of the nineteenth century has been faithfully reconstructed.

29 __ Ghost Hill
Spooky Town

Belief in ghosts is widespread in Japan. Across the country there are many places called Yurei-zaka (Ghost Hill), including at least eight in Tokyo alone. Each of these haunted elevations has its own mythology.

The best-known ghost hill in the capital is the one in Mita 4-Chome. It is associated with two legends that compete for the reader's attention. One of these says that the shogun Iemitsu Tokugawa developed this area to expand his power in the seventeenth century. He transferred several temples and shrines, as well as military installations, to the area. His daimyo (feudal lords) also pitched their tents on the new road. In those days, the district was deserted and densely wooded. It was gloomy even during the day, and pitch black at night. In these hours, it was only possible to travel along the road on nights when the moon was bright enough to light the way. It was the ideal place for thieves and ghosts to lie in wait for unwitting passers-by and fall upon them.

According to another legend, a man who lived in the area 200 years later, during the Meiji period, attracted the ghosts to Mita. His name was Arinori Mori (森有礼), and he was both a leading thinker and a disputatious man. Spiteful persons called him yurei (ghost), because his name could be read with this meaning. Mori studied in London, becoming the first Japanese ambassador to the USA (1870–1873) and later the first minister of education in the Meiji government. After his return, he planned to reform the education system on the American model. He argued for replacing the Japanese language with English. He also campaigned in favour of the free practice of religion and supported the extension of rights for women. For many of his contemporaries, these anglophile opinions were much too revolutionary. The end of the story was inevitable: in 1889 Mori was assassinated.

Address 幽霊坂, Yurei-zaka, Mita 4-12-18, Minato-ku, 108−0073 Tokyo | **Getting there** Nanboku metro line to Shirokane-takanawa, 7-minute walk | **Tip** If you would like to take a ghost tour yourself, the Haunted Tokyo Tours are recommended. Expert guides take you to the spookiest places in the city at the midnight hour (www.hauntedtokyotours.com).

30_ The Golf Course Simulator

Today the Fuji Classic, tomorrow St Andrews

Golf is one of the most popular sports in Japan. Among office workers it is the undisputed number one. However, membership of a golf club is extremely expensive, and therefore restricted to wealthy people. The less privileged do their training on one of the numerous driving ranges, which are hidden away behind high fences of wire mesh. As an alternative to this, there are golf simulators which, thanks to technology that is getting better all the time, give players the impression that they are out on a real golf course.

One of the best simulators is at inGOLF in Ikebukuro. Here you can train as often as you like and whenever you like, regardless of the weather or the time of day: this school of golf is open round the clock. You decide for yourself whether you agree fixed times for the training sessions or squeeze them into your crowded diary at short notice. From the correct posture and the best way to hold the clubs to the perfect swing, whether your preference is for a wood, an iron or a putter – you can take lessons in all of these categories every day of the week. Two high-speed cameras record how you tee off. This allows you to watch your swing exactly and thus make a diagnosis of your weaknesses. No matter whether you are a complete beginner or working your way to a single-figure handicap, inGOLF caters for every level of ability. For people who are unsure whether this is the right sport for them, free trial lessons are on offer.

Are you worried that training with a computer might become monotonous? It is nothing of the kind. At the start of the lesson you decide yourself where you are going to play. Do you feel like trying the Fuji Classic in Yamanashi, or has it always been your dream to play a round at St Andrews? At inGOLF you have the choice: simulations of more than 180 golf courses all over the world are at your disposal.

Address inGOLF, 2F, Ikebukuro-Honcho 2-7-5, Toshima-ku, 170–0011 Tokyo, +81 (0) 359 577 003, www.in-golf.jp | **Getting there** Tobu Line to Kita-Ikebukuro, 10-minute walk | **Tip** In the same building is the Don Quijote store. It is very popular amongst young Japanese, and sells bargain items.

31__The Gotokuji Temple

From stray tomcat to hero

The figure of a luck-bringing white cat waving its paw is well-known around the world. There are different legends about when and where it first appeared. A widely accepted version, which sounds like a fairy tale but for which there is said to be written evidence, maintains that the maneki-neko originated in the seventeenth century in the Gotokuji Temple in Setagaya.

The priest of the temple, which was a very poor institution in those days, took in a white tomcat, even though he scarcely had enough to eat himself, and gave it the name Tama. It was with a heavy heart that he sent the cat away when his money problems grew even worse. But Tama did not go far.

One day, as a storm was approaching, the faithful animal was sitting by the roadside close to the temple. A samurai and his servant, who were passing by on the road, took shelter from the rain beneath a tree. When they noticed the cat, it raised its paw, as if it wanted to give them a sign. They interpreted this gesture correctly and hurriedly left their place of shelter. At the moment they reached the cat, a bolt of lightning hit the tree. Happy events then took their course. Grateful to the animal that had saved his life, the samurai became a patron of the temple and provided it with generous donations. Financial problems were now a thing of the past, and Tama became the showpiece and mascot of the Gotokuji Temple.

When he died, he was buried in the cemetery of this religious site, and a statue of a waving cat was set up to honour him. News of this tale spread like wildfire, and people began to place figures of waving cats in their homes, too. They believed that this would bring good fortune and prosperity. The Gotokuji Temple exists to this day. There is no longer only a single statue of the prescient tomcat, set up there long ago – since then hundreds more have been added to it.

Address 豪徳寺, Gotokuji Temple, Gotokuji 2-24-7, Setagaya-ku, 154–0021 Tokyo | **Getting there** Setagaya tram line to Miya-no-Saka, 6-minute walk | **Tip** Close to the Miya-no-Saka train station lies the Hachimangu Shrine. Here there is a sumo ring, where sumo wrestling contests are held at a festival in September.

32___The Grave of an Idol
The mysterious death of Yutaka Ozaki

The last resting place of the rock singer and songwriter Yutaka Ozaki (29.11.1965 – 25.4.1992), who died way too young at the age of 26, is in the Sayamakohan-Reien cemetery in rural surroundings in Tokorozawa. It is not a normal grave. Many fans who make the pilgrimage there on Ozaki's birthday or the day of his death take cigarettes with them rather than incense. He liked smoking. The outsized gravestone bears the following inscription: 'Say yes to life. Every day!' This is both the singer's motto and the title of one of his songs.

Ozaki kept faith with this motto – to the very end. In the mid-1980s he became an idol for young Japanese people. He found words to express the feelings of his generation, singing of affection, shame and despair. The rebellion of the young against their parents, whose conformity they felt was restricting them, was also a theme. Ozaki could not cope with his fame, however, and sought refuge in drugs. In 1987 he got into trouble with the law and was sent to prison for two months for possession of illegal substances. He was often described as the Japanese Kurt Cobain.

On 25 April, 1992 he was found naked in a front garden in Adachi following heavy consumption of drugs and alcohol, and died the same day. The official cause of death was given as 'edema of the lung resulting from drug abuse'.

Despite his colourful past, neither the family nor the record company believed that Ozaki had brought about his own death. They were convinced that he had been forced to take the drugs. Directly after Ozaki's death, doubt also arose in the media. This could be taken as an indication that information was withheld from the public. 100,000 signatures were collected for a petition calling for the cause of death to be re-examined. However, the exact circumstances of the tragedy will never be known.

生きるこ そ れ は 日々を告白してゆくことだろう

—放熱への証—

尾崎

Address 尾崎豊の墓, 狭山湖畔霊園, Ozaki Yutaka-no-Haka, Sayamakohan-Reien,
Kami-Yamaguchi 2050, 359–1153 Tokorozawa | Getting there Seibu-Sayama Line to
Seibu-Kyujo-mae, 10-minute walk | Tip Between the train stations Seibu-Kyujo-mae and
Seibu-Yuenchi, there runs a shuttle, the Leo Liner. Its 2.8-kilometre route passes a golf
course and travels through lovely countryside.

33__Hachijo-jima Island
Japan's Hawaii?

In the 1960s there were plans to develop the island of Hachijo-jima for tourism and turn it into 'Japan's Hawaii'. An indication of the failure of this tourism campaign is a huge hotel that was left to decay. In 2004 the luxury accommodation was closed, and is now one of Japan's three biggest ruins.

Today this volcanic island in the Pacific Ocean has a lonely and neglected appearance. Geographically it is one of the Izu Islands, and although it lies at a distance of 278 kilometres from the capital city, administratively it belongs to Tokyo. The crossing by ship takes ten hours, and by air you can reach the island in 50 minutes. Hachijo-jima has an area of approximately 60 square kilometres and a population of a little over 8,000. The climate is subtropical, and the vegetation, including palm trees, hibiscus, bougainvillea and many other plants, is like something from paradise. There are two volcanic mountains. The taller one, Nishi-Yama, is 854 metres high, and known as Hachijo-Fuji. The neighbouring island, Hachijo-Kojima, seven kilometres away, is connected to Hachijo-jima by ferry.

From the Edo period until the end of the Meiji period, prisoners were exiled to Hachijo-jima. Both respected daimyo – the best-known of whom was Hideie Ukita, who lost the Battle of Sekigahara – and common prisoners were deported to the island, which seems never to have completely succeeded in shaking off its negative image. Not only did tourists stay away, but many fishermen and farmers, who mostly lived on the smaller neighbouring island of Hachijo-Kojima, emigrated for economic reasons.

The island never became a second Hawaii. The upside of this is that it has kept its natural charm. The volcanic landscape is fascinating, especially the wide-ranging view of Hachijo-Kojima from the lava field on the beach. It is paradise for lovers of nature and lost places.

Address Island Government Office, Okago 2345-1, 100–1401 Hachijo-machi, 八丈島, Hachijo Island | Getting there Information is available at www.wikitravel.org/en/Hachijojima | Tip From Sokodo beach near the ferry harbour you can go snorkelling and diving. There are corals and tropical fish, and with a little luck you might see a few turtles.

34_ The High-Class Butcher
Waiting for the city's best beef

Kobe beef is said to be the best in the world. Less well-known abroad, but no less exclusive, is Matsuzaka beef. It comes from a breed of black cows that is bred in the Matsuzaka area in Mie Prefecture, and nowhere else. It is characterised by densely marbled, fine veins of fat, which ensure that the meat is particularly tender and aromatic.

Matsuzaka cows are extremely well cared for. They live in idyllic surroundings and are fed a varied diet. If they don't feel hungry, their appetite is stimulated with beer. Regular massage is also part of the treatment. This labour-intensive care comes at a price: a 250-gram slice of steak costs around 10,000 yen.

Even in Japan the opportunities to enjoy such exquisite meat are few and far between. Kichijoji-Sato is among the old established companies that are specialised in Matsuzaka beef. As this butcher buys direct from the breeder, without any middleman, prices there are usually a little lower than those of other suppliers. In addition to this speciality, which is mostly sold in the form of paper-thin slices, a further popular product is menchikatsu, croquettes filled with minced beef.

This butcher's shop opened for business back in 1948, and for no less than 30 years in succession was voted the best specialist supplier of Matsuzaka beef in the whole of Japan. The word has spread, and Kichijoji-Sato has built up a base of quality-conscious customers. Following renovation work carried out a few years ago, there is a steakhouse above the shop. Here the fine meat from Matsuzaka cows is prepared by expert professional chefs. If you come for an evening meal it is possible to book by telephone. At midday, expect to wait in a queue for some time, as you normally have to do in the butcher's shop. Although online shopping is now possible, many customers prefer to come and buy their beef in person.

Address 吉祥寺さとう, Kichijoji-Sato, Kichijoji Honcho 1-1-8, Musashino-shi, 180–0004 Tokyo, +81 (0) 422 223 130 | **Getting there** JR-Chuo Line to Kichijoji | **Hours** Shop: daily 10am–7pm | **Tip** When the Ichien ramen restaurant opened close to the station, a portion cost one yen, which explains the name. It is no longer quite so cheap, but the old atmosphere remains.

35__Hillside Terrace
Slow but sure

In view of the chaotic way the city has been built, you might suppose that there is no urban planning in Japan. However, a plethora of regulations does impose restrictions such as the maximum height allowed for a building. On the other hand, scarce attention is paid to whether the houses in a section of street match each other. It therefore sometimes happens that developers buy several plots of land and erect new residential blocks or office towers that do not fit in with their surroundings at all.

Fortunately there are exceptions: Daikanyama, today a fashionable district, was still almost rural in the late 1960s. The old-established Asakura family wanted to develop its estates and commissioned Fumihiko Maki, later holder of the Pritzker Prize, for the purpose. As the family did not want to be exposed to large financial risks, together with Maki they planned the project in several phases.

The six stages of construction thus lasted more than 25 years, from the start of planning in 1967 until completion of the last complex in 1992. After each phase everything was re-evaluated in order to enable the best possible planning for the next stage. The result is a homogeneous and at the same time highly varied ensemble of buildings, containing shops, homes, offices, places to eat and drink and exhibition spaces, which also fits well aesthetically in its surroundings.

There is no designated way of exploring the complex, but its individual parts are marked alphabetically. It is a good idea to follow this classification. You can pass through buildings or walk around them. Going up steps and along passages, you are presented with constantly changing prospects of courtyards, gardens, rows of shops and much more. The Danish embassy is also located here. Nevertheless, the site is structured to provide orientation, so that there is no danger of losing your way.

Address ヒルサイドテラス, Hillside Terrace, Sarugaku-cho 18-8, Shibuya-ku, 150−0033 Tokyo, www.hillsideterrace.com | **Getting there** Tokyu-Toyoko Line (local) to Daikanyama, 3-minute walk | **Hours** The site is always accessible, while individual opening hours vary. | **Tip** Behind Hillside Terrace, when seen from the road, is the old residence of the Asakura family. This building with a garden, dating from 1919, is now a museum and an interesting contrast to the modern complex designed by the architect Maki in which the Asakura family lives today.

36__ The Hobbit Village

From a hippie commune to vegetable business

One of the first alternative department stores in Japan was founded in 1976 by the Nagamoto brothers, who called it Hobbit-Mura (Hobbit Village). The three-storey building in Nishi-Ogikubo houses several shops, a restaurant and a free school under one roof. Here the mindful consumer can find everything that is necessary to lead a healthy lifestyle.

The food shop Umai-Yaoya on the ground floor sells organic vegetables, while the workshop called Studio-Jam on the same floor specialises in furniture and interiors for the environmentally aware. Café Balthazar on the first floor serves healthy Japanese meals. The changing daily menu (Higawari lunch) is recommended: in addition to a main course it includes a miso soup, whole-grain rice, salad and several small side dishes. It does not matter what you choose: everything tastes delicious. On the top floor is an alternative bookshop, Nawa-Plazad, where the focus is on literature about alternative ways of life. You will also find a good selection of healing and new-age music here. Regular workshops and talks are held in the classrooms of the free school after the day's lessons are over.

Hobbit-Mura is more than just a place to go shopping. It is also a kind of information centre for critically minded citizens. Namo, one of the Nagamoto brothers, was one of Japan's few active hippies when he was a young man. His group gave itself the name Buzoku (trunk or stem). He lived with the other members of the group in a secluded commune on an island in the south of the country.

Back in those days, he was one of the first Japanese to practise organic vegetable farming. The thoroughly self-sufficient lifestyle of the commune impressed even American hippies. Internationally recognised icons of the movement such as Allen Ginsberg and Gary Snyder made repeated visits in order to gain inspiration.

Address ホビット村, Hobbit-Mura, Nishiogi-Minami 3-15-3, Suginami-ku, 167–0053 Tokyo, +81 (0) 333 313 599, www.nabra.co.jp/hobbit/hobbit_mura.htm | Getting there JR-Chuo Line (local) to Nishi-Ogikubo, 3-minute walk | Hours Vary according to the different shops | Tip The Ogikubo quarter is famous for its excellent ramen restaurants.

37 __ The Home of FC Tokyo
A club with a soul

In the country that hosted the World Cup in 2002, enthusiasm for football was limited for many years. One reason for this lack of interest is that support for the sport was neglected. The Japan Professional Soccer League was not founded until 1992. As the quality of the players on the field improved, the number of fans also grew. Today the J-League is one of the most successful competitions in Asia.

As far as football in the capital of Japan is concerned, the positions of the two leading clubs are very different. FC Tokyo doggedly remain in the mid-to-lower reaches of the first division, and had their best results in 2003 and 2015, holding fourth place in those years. Tokyo Verdy play in the second division, and are not particularly successful there.

FC Tokyo originated in 1935 as a company team: the Tokyo Gas Football Club. In 1998 companies including TEPCO and TV Tokyo began to sponsor the club, founding the Tokyo Football Club Company. Following the appointment of Hiromi Hara as manager in 2002, the first successes were achieved.

The team's famous players at that time were the Brazilian Amara, known to his fans as the 'king of Tokyo', and later Yasuyuki Konno, who was a member of the Japanese national team at the Olympic Games in Athens in 2004. The fans' great favourite at FC Tokyo, until he moved to play for FSV Mainz 05 in the German Bundesliga in 2015, was Yoshinori Muto.

In a contest to find the best-loved club mascot in 2016, FC Tokyo took second place. Their lucky mascot is called Dorampa and looks like a raccoon dog. The first-team players in their red-and-blue kit can only dream of such a position in the league at present. Nevertheless, the Tokyo club has the highest home attendances, apart from Urawa Reds from Saitama. The Ajinomoto Stadium in Fuchu has capacity for 50,000 spectators, who give noisy encouragement to their team: 'Gambare FC Tokyo!'

Address 味の素スタジアム, Ajinomoto-Stadium, Nishi-Machi 376-3, Chofu-shi, 182–0032 Tokyo, www.fctokyo.co.jp/english | **Getting there** Keio Line to Tobitakyu, 7-minute walk | **Tip** Since it was renovated, the train station at Tobitakyu has regained its old sparkle and been fitted with modern design—a fine architectural sight!

38_ The Hot Spring

Where body and soul recuperate

Nothing is more relaxing than spending some time in an onsen. All over Japan, tours can be booked for visits to spas that have this kind of thermal bath.

If a busy schedule does not leave you time to undertake such a journey, there are a number of hot springs in Tokyo too where you can pass a leisurely day. An especially recommended bathhouse is Yumori-no-Sato in Musashino.

For the owner of this onsen it is important that guests should feel at home. For this reason the rooms were fitted out for a cosy mood using a lot of wood, in accordance with the principles of feng shui. Here you can also choose from a wide assortment of therapeutic massages and cosmetic treatments. Cushions and futons are available in the rest zone for relaxation after the bath. In the restaurant, which serves après-onsen dishes, you can round off a day of health and beauty treatments in a pleasant atmosphere.

The water in the bath comes from a hot spring, far below the earth's surface at a depth of 1,500 metres. It gets its characteristic dark colour from plant material that is found there, which is derived from common bracken and seaweed. A high proportion of humic acid ensures that the mineral content of the water is not lost. This acid is said to assist in breaking down toxic substances in the body. For this reason the water is used in its natural condition without any chemical additions at Yumori-no-Sato. Only minimal quantities of chlorine are used for the purpose of disinfection. Regular visitors to this onsen swear by the healing properties of this water. The hot spring of Yumori-no-Sato is said to have beneficial effects in cases of ailments related to the nervous system and muscles, to osteo-arthritis and problems with blood circulation. After taking a bath here you will feel wonderfully restored and will return to everyday life with a fresh supply of energy.

Address 湯守の里, Yumori-no-Sato, Jindaiji-Motomachi 2-12-2, Chofu-shi,
182–0017 Tokyo, +81 (0) 424 997 777, www.yumorinosato.com | Getting there JR-Chuo
Line (local) to Musashino-Sakai, south exit; a free shuttle bus leaves from the station once
every hour | Hours Daily 10am–10pm | Tip Jindai-Ji, 10 minutes on foot from the onsen,
was built in the seventh century and is Tokyo's second-oldest temple. The nearby restaurants
serve jindai-ji-soba, a noodle soup made with local fresh water.

39__The House of Taikan Yokoyama

A painter who was ahead of his time

Taikan Yokoyama (1868–1958) was one of the most important figures in the history of Japanese painting. The house in Ueno in which he lived for a long time, and where he painted many of his works, is open to visitors today.

The artist's real name was Hidemaro Sakai. He came from Mito in Ibaragi Prefecture. He travelled to far-away places, including the United States and European countries, in search of inspiration, experiemented with Western painting techniques and reformed traditional Japanese painting. With another artist, Shunso Hishida, Yokoyama developed the Morotai style: instead of working with brushstrokes, the outlines were blurred. In his later career Yokoyama specialised in monochrome ink drawings, and so went down in history as the 'master of shades of grey'.

The artist's endeavours to achieve innovation and in particular the invention of the Morotai style are the reasons why Yokoyama was greatly admired after his death, receiving many awards. During his lifetime, however, he was frequently too revolutionary from the point of view of his critics. Nevertheless, he always remained true to his principles and never allowed himself to depart from a course on which he had set out. He was not an easy man. On several occasions in his artistic career he was employed in a public position as a teacher or as a member of a selection committee, but more than once he resigned his post prematurely as a result of conflicts.

Yokoyama moved into his house in Ueno in 1909 and lived there until his death. When the home was destroyed by an air raid in 1945, he moved temporarily to his holiday house in Atami on the Izu Peninsula. Yokoyama rebuilt a new house based on the construction plans of the old one, and returned to live in it in 1954.

Address 横山大観記念館, Yokoyama Taikan Memorial Hall, Ike-no-Hata 1-4-24, Taito-ku, 110−0008 Tokyo, +81 (0) 338 211 017, taikan.tokyo/English.html | **Getting there** Chiyoda metro line to Yushima, 7-minute walk | **Hours** Thu−Sun 10am−4pm (closed during summer and winter holidays) | **Tip** Kyu-Iwasaki-Tei-Teien is a garden near Ueno Park. The estate once belonged to the Iwasaki family, the founders of the Mitsubishi company.

40 Kaminoge Station

A small station by a great architect

Japanese train stations are usually rather humdrum. It only gets interesting when you try to change trains in a large station where several lines are operated by different companies: as every rail company has its own station with its own entrances and exits, the connections between them are often like a maze. As far as architecture is concerned, this is often not very stimulating unless you take a liking to improvisation in old buildings, where bundles of cables visibly snake along the ceilings and walls like aliens.

This makes the pleasure all the greater when you come across a station as attractive as the one in Kaminoge. This is merely a local station, with only a single line and no connections to express trains. As the functional old building was not accessible to people with handicaps, a new one had to be built. The Japanese architect who is best known internationally, Tadao Ando, was chosen to design it. Ando is known for his minimalist style with clear lines in exposed concrete and glass. He had already designed several stations, including, in Tokyo, the underground station for the Tokyu Lines in Shibuya and the station at Ryuo on the Chuo-Honsen Line.

The approach by train and the first impression when you alight are not especially interesting: the walls parallel to the tracks have an uninterrupted line of windows extending the entire length of the building, which bathe the simple platform in natural light. But at the main exit, the design is livelier: here you step out on to a road that divides the station building located above the rail tracks. However, the two parts share a roof, which spans the road and thus shelters the bus stops on both sides from rain. This special method of construction made it necessary to renovate the station in 2016, even though it had only been built five years earlier, but it has now regained its fresh appearance once again.

Address 上野毛駅, Kaminoge-Station, Kaminoge 1-26-6, Setagaya-ku, 158–0093 Tokyo | **Getting there** Tokyu-Oimachi Line (local) to Kaminoge | **Tip** Anbaru Café, immediately south of the station, served various kinds of coffee long before the big chains muscled in. The cosy, old-fashioned atmosphere here is now unusual in Japan.

41_ The Kanayama Shrine

The story of a jealous demon

Thanks to the fertility festival, which is celebrated every year on the first Sunday in April and culminates in a procession, when a portable shrine with a gigantic phallus is carried through the streets of Kawasaki by transvestites, the Kanayama Shrine is already well known. The story behind this religious site is, however, not familiar to many people.

In the sixteenth century, courtesans went to the shrine in supplication, asking the gods to protect them from sexually transmitted diseases. As many travelling merchants stopped over in Kawasaki on their way to Edo, prostitution was a flourishing business there.

According to a legend, a malevolent demon took up residence in the vagina of a young girl after it found out that she was due to be married. The demon was determined to prevent the marriage, and on the wedding night it bit off the penis of the newly betrothed husband. The same dramatic fate befell the girl's second husband. To put a stop to this devilry, an ingenious blacksmith came up with a plan: to trick the demon with the help of a metal phallus. The ruse was successful, and the demon, injured and ashamed, fled from his hiding place. The inventive smith was then permitted to marry the girl. Since that day, the phallus has been the symbol of the Kanayama Shrine, and in memory of the brave man who drove out the demon, a huge metal penis was placed in the grounds of the sanctuary.

Today the hope of fertility is the main reason that people come to the shrine. They write down their wishes on wooden tablets known as ema and hang them up at the shrine. The figure depicted on the ema is a Japanese hero called Momotaro. He was the son of an old couple who were denied the good fortune of having children of their own. The boy Momotaro hatched from a peach that his elderly mother had found in a river.

Address 金山神社, Kanayama-Shrine, Daishi-Eki-mae 2-13-16, Kawasaki-ku, 210–0802 Kawasaki | **Getting there** Keikyu-Daishi Line to Kawasaki-Daishi, 3-minute walk | **Tip** On the grounds of the Kanayama Shrine is a small museum with many exhibits about the history of the shrine. Traditional souvenirs and Japanese sweets are sold in the shopping street Nakamise-Dori.

42__Kawanone

Meals that relax you

In Tokyo it is rare to leave a restaurant disappointed, and it is well worth setting off on culinary journeys of discovery. Even if you cannot read a Japanese menu, helpful staff are almost always at hand to provide an English translation of the day's dishes.

If you would like to celebrate a special occasion – whether it is a romantic dinner for two or a larger-scale event – and are looking for a place with a special atmosphere, Kawanone in Akasaka is recommended. The name means 'the rushing of the river', and this is part of the concept. A Japanese garden, through which a little stream meanders, has been created in the dark interior. The splashing sound of the waterfall has a calming effect. On the restaurant's homepage, the owner promises a meal with a 'healing effect' for stressed city dwellers. Guests who prefer to enjoy their meal in absolutely peaceful surroundings may telephone in advance to book a private dining area.

Not only the interior of Kawanone makes a good impression. You are sure to be satisfied with the quality of the cooking. The menu holds a wide range of Japanese culinary treats in store. You can choose from tofu dishes, vegetable snacks, fish and meat dishes and from many other delights. In addition to various classics, you will also find out-of-the-ordinary offerings that are definitely worth trying. Don't miss the roasted ginkgo fruit, which literally melts in the mouth, or the deep-fried salsify sticks. If you would like to enjoy a few surprises from the selection that the kitchen produces, the best option is to order a set menu.

The prices start at about 3,500 yen. An all-inclusive offer is especially to be recommended if you would like to take an alcoholic drink with your meal, as this is relatively expensive in Japan. Dining here costs less at midday, when set lunch menus are available from 1,000 yen.

Address 川の音, Kawanone B 1, Akasaka 3-13-4, Minato-ku, 107–0052 Tokyo, +81 (0) 366 597 608, www.kawanone.net/reserve (only Japanese) | Getting there Marunouchi metro line and others to Akasaka-Mitsuke, 8-minute walk | Hours Mon–Fri 11.30am–2pm and 4.30–11.30pm (last orders 11pm), Sat, Sun & public holidays 4.30–11pm | Tip Akasaka is a lively district with a lot of bars, a good area to go for a drink after a meal.

43__Kikumatsuya
Cosy Japanese style with a touch of Osaka

Many Japanese have an ambiguous attitude to old things: on the one hand, they appreciate cultural heritage if it is officially recognised, but otherwise anything that is old is regarded as 'dirty' and is thought best avoided. For example, in a restaurant many people don't simply place their bags on the floor, but put them in baskets specially provided for the purpose. If desired, you can do this in Kikumatsuya.

It may seem a contradiction that this izakaya (Japanese pub) occupies a wooden building that dates from the early post-war years. In Japan this is already regarded as old, as anything that has stood for 40 years is usually demolished. This building was constructed in a traditional architectural style that used to dominate the urban scene everywhere in Japan but is now increasingly disappearing. Although almost nobody wants to live in a house like this, pubs in old buildings have charm and a touch of nostalgia. When he opened in 2009, the landlord, Tsutomu Nagata from Osaka, left nothing to chance in restoring the premises to their old glory. Even the large bar counter in the front room has been made from old sliding doors. Guests in the back room sit on ancient wooden benches taken from a school.

In this cosy atmosphere, Nagata displays his skills as a cook, with the food changing according to the season. As portions are usually small in an izakaya, you can sample a broad range of Japanese dishes: sashimi (fish or horse), grilled skewers, udon noodles and oden (a kind of hotpot) are all on offer.

If you sit at the bar at the front, you will get an impression of Osaka, as Mr Nagata likes to talk to his guests – in English too – and introduces them to each other, which gives them the feeling of being in a kind of public living room.

This is quite different from the more reserved manner of Tokyo people.

Address 菊松屋, Kikumatsuya, Takamatsu-cho 2-1-23, Tachikawa-shi, 190−0011 Tokyo, +81 (0) 425 267 583, www.kikumatsuya.com (only Japanese) | **Getting there** JR-Chuo Line and others to Tachikawa, 10-minute walk | **Hours** Mon−Sat 5.30pm−midnight | **Tip** Before a meal at Kikumatsuya you can go to the Tachikawa-Keirinjo velodrome and try to boost your meal budget by betting on the races.

44__Koichiro Kimura House

Inspired by the ancient Egyptians

Design at the highest degree of perfection is to be found at Maison Koichiro Kimura in Aoyama. The owner of the gallery comes from a family that has been making traditional lacquer wares (urushi) for 400 years. Mr Kimura's true wish was to become a fashion designer, but in the end he kept faith with the family company. In his work there, he is not content producing lacquered tableware according to the old tradition, but strives to innovate.

Kimura's range of artistic activities is immeasurable. They range from decoration of small items of everyday use to furniture and the design of whole rooms. He likes to exchange ideas on an international level, and in Gucci, Vogue and Meissen found partners for cooperation that focus on good design.

A hallmark of his works is shapes and surfaces, often in white, that have an unmistakable structure. From a distance, the surface looks like the pattern on a waffle, but from close up you perceive small pyramidal blocks that are made in a similar way to lacquered tableware. This design is applied in the so-called Pharaoh series, in which the interplay of light and shade creates a 3-D effect. Sometimes he adds a small touch by designing only one element, for example the leg of a table, in the pyramid style, but sometimes the walls of a room are partly or completely clad in this way.

You can get your own impression of the effect of this pattern at Maison Koichiro Kimura in Aoyama. On the upper floor of the building is a showroom, decorated entirely in the design of the Pharaoh series. 4,000 white pyramidal blocks were made for the purpose. The sales room is on the ground floor. Here, the interior design concentrates on essentials. The eye-catching feature is a white wall that looks like a cloud. The maestro sits behind it. Sometimes he suddenly appears in the sales room, like a ninja who walks through walls.

Address 木村 浩一郎, Maison Koichiro Kimura, Jingumae 5-3-12, Shibuya-ku, 150–0001 Tokyo, +81 (0) 364 274 877, www.koichiro-kimura.com | **Getting there** Ginza metro line to Omotesando, exit A 1, 4-minute walk | **Hours** Daily 11am–8pm | **Tip** The nearby shopping centre Omotesando Hills is a work of the famous architect Tadao Ando. It was built in the style of Tokyo's oldest residential block, which had previously been demolished.

45 __ Komazawa Olympic Park
Fleeing with James Bond

At present the Japanese capital is being smartened up for the Olympic Games in 2020. Tokyo was an Olympic venue for the first time in 1964. The city would have taken its turn earlier, in 1940, but the outbreak of the Second World War prevented the staging of the games. A reminder of this period is the Komazawa Olympic Park in the Setagaya district.

Today this site is a popular place for people who like to take exercise. On an area of 41 hectares there are several sports fields, as well as biking and running tracks. For families with children, the attractions are playgrounds and a zoo with pigs and squirrels.

Around Chuo-Hiroba, the central square of the park, is a row of architectural works that were built for the Olympic Games in summer 1964. At the upper end is a tower of reinforced concrete, 50 metres high, in a blue-tiled pool, the Olympic-Kinen-To. Its striking shape is reminiscent of a Japanese pagoda. A little further on you come to the Komazawa Gymnasium, an impressive, circular indoor sports hall. From a distance, its pointed roof structure resembles a paper hat. Both of these buildings are works by the architect Yoshinobu Ashihara (1918–2003). The Rikujokyogijo, the athletics stadium, also catches the eye of visitors immediately. A roof designed in the shape of a petal protects spectators in the stands from the sun and rain. The architect Masachika Murata (1906–1987) was commissioned to plan this, the largest arena in the Olympic park.

If this odd-looking site should seem somehow vaguely familiar to you, the reason might be that you recognise it from an old James Bond film. When Sean Connery played the role of Bond in *You Only Live Twice* (1967) and fled from the city in a scene with a beautiful Japanese woman, the Komazawa Olympic Park was visible in the background.

Address 駒沢オリンピック公園, Komazawa-Olympic-Koen, Komazawa-Koen 1–1, Setagaya-ku, 154–0013 Tokyo | Getting there Tokyu-Denentoshi Line (local) to Komazawa-Daigaku, 10-minute walk | Tip It is worth visiting the Zen Buddhism Museum on the campus of Komazawa University. The architecture, too, is interesting. It dates from the 1920s, and was built in a fine Expressionist style.

46 _ The Korean Quarter
Seoul food and attractive men

In 2002 the South Korean television series Fuyu no Sonata (A Winter Sonata) was shown on Japanese channels in the morning. The youthful stars of this soap opera attained the status of heroes, especially among middle-aged Japanese women. There was a remarkable boom in hanryu, as this trend from South Korea was called. Business people in Korean Town, the Korean quarter in Shin-Okubo, did a roaring trade.

In numerous fan shops, items connected with the series sold like hot cakes. Not only that: the district as a whole became a trendy location, and hopes were expressed in the media that the two countries, whose relationship had been difficult for a long time, could come closer through pop culture. However, the way with trends is that enthusiasm peters out as quickly as it first appeared, and this was the case here too. Pop music from the Asian neighbour, known for short as K-pop, is still played, but the soap opera was simply too kitschy to keep a permanent following.

When the run was over, it was very quiet in the Korean quarter for several years, and most of the fan shops gave way to other stores. Today the streets of Korean Town are livelier again. The low-cost and highly recommended restaurants of the district and the supermarkets that sell everything you need to cook Korean meals are doing good business again.

The centre of the district is around the streets Okubo-Dori and Shokuan-Dori, and in the connecting alley that is popularly known simply as Ikemen-Dori (Street of the Attractive Men). It gets its unusual name from an establishment in the lane, Kohi-Purinsu (Café Prince), which is also the name of a Korean series. The rumour that this café is always frequented by extremely attractive men has taken a firm hold. Who needs Korean soap operas when you can go there and meet hunky guys from Seoul in person?

Address コリアン・タウン, Korean-Town, Hyakunincho 1-10, Shinjuku-ku, 169–0073 Tokyo | **Getting there** JR-Yamanote Line to Shin-Okubo | **Tip** One of the most popular restaurants in Korean Town is Derikaondoru. Traditional dishes such as hotpot, barbecues and omelettes are served there.

47___The Kurosawa
The fantastical world of Akira Kurosawa

This place is warmly recommended to all fans of the internationally renowned film-maker Akira Kurosawa. Immediately after his death in 1988, the film crew decided to commemorate their beloved boss with a monument. It was to be a restaurant, as Kurosawa had a weakness for eating well. His favourite foods included selected Japanese meat dishes and soba noodles. Both of these are prepared in the kitchen of Kurosawa in such a way that the maestro would have enjoyed them. For the interior decoration, sets from his well-known films Red Beard and Yojimba were recreated. A further highlight is a replica of samurai armour from Shadow Warrior. The walls are hung with photos of Kurosawa, old movie posters and hand-painted film sketches that Kurosawa, a talented artist, always drew himself.

The restaurant is on two floors. On the ground floor, à la carte meals and a simple fixed menu are served. On the upper floor is a room in genuine Japanese style with tables, beneath which the floor has been opened up to make space for diners' legs. In this way guests can enjoy traditional surroundings without having to endure a cross-legged position.

On the upper floor special dishes are served. They include steak, turtle soup and shabu-shabu, wafer-thin slices of meat that are cooked for no more than a few seconds at the table in water. The menu changes every month. The prices on the ground floor start at around 1,000 yen for a soba menu. On the upper floor, too, lunch menus are on offer, and at much lower prices than for dinner in the evening.

This little traditional of the great film director is situated in Nagatacho, at the heart of the political district of the city, surrounded by modern palaces of glass that are home to the offices of member of parliament, luxury hotels and lawyers' chambers. There could hardly be a starker contrast than this.

Address 黒澤, Kurosawa, Nagata-cho 2-7-9, Chiyoda-ku, 100-0014 Tokyo, +81 (03) 35 809 638, www.9638.net/nagata (only in Japanese) | Getting there Chiyoda and Marunouchi Line to Kokkaigijido-mae, exit no. 5, 1-minute walk | Hours Mon–Fri 11.30am–3pm & 5–11pm, Sat & holidays noon–10pm | Tip Only 300 metres away is the Hie shrine, founded by Prince Dokan Ota in the 15th century for the patron deity of Edo. Today you can reach it in comfort on an escalator.

48 The Last Fuji Hill
The lost view

In the centre of Tokyo there used to be many hills that gave a view of Mount Fuji, 100 kilometres away, when the weather conditions were right. These places were named fujimizaka (elevation with a view of Fuji). As the urban jungle became denser and denser, and skyscrapers rose higher and higher into the sky, these opportunities to get a glimpse of the Japanese landmark from ground level disappeared one by one.

For a long time, the fujimizaka between the Nippori and Nishi-Nippori train stations in the Arakawa district was the last hill that still lived up to its name. The local residents did all they could to preserve their view of the world's most beautiful silhouette, but they were destined to lose their fight against profit-seeking real estate companies.

At the beginning of the millennium, it was all over for the idyllic view in Nippori. In 1999 a subsidiary of the steel corporation Nippon Kokan (NKK) started construction of a 13-storey block of apartments in Bunkyo, the neighbouring district. The residents of Nippori founded a citizens' campaign to get it reduced to nine storeys. In vain. Failing to build the top four floors would allegedly have meant losses for the developer. Since the building was completed, it has blocked the view of the left side of Fuji. And worse was to come: in 2011 the property giant Sumitomo-Fudosan bought land in Okubo, six kilometres distant as the crow flies, and decided to build a 160-metre skyscraper there.

This plan was clearly going to spoil the very last opportunity to enjoy the view of Mount Fuji from ground level in the city centre, leaving only the option of looking from a tall building. Despite the untiring efforts of the citizens' campaign, construction went ahead, and the battle for the last viewpoint was lost. Which goes to show that Tokyo is not a place for sentimental attitudes.

Address 日暮里の富士見坂, Nippori-no-Fujimizaka, Nishi-Nippori 3-7, Arakawa-ku, 116–0013 Tokyo | Getting there JR-Yamanote Line to Nishi-Nippori, 5-minute walk | Tip The Asakura Choso Museum, 7-minute walk away, was the house of the sculptor Fumio Asakura (1883–1964). It contrasts starkly with that of the painter Taikan Yokoyama, which is presented later in this book.

冬の朝は真っ白な富士山が良く見える （2002年2月）

日が沈むと富士山はシルエットに （1999年1月）
―この時はまだ左稜線が見えていた―

49___The Leprosy Museum
A belated cry for justice

In the film *Sweet Bean*, the director Naomi Kawase sensitively tells the story of an old lady whose hands are deformed by leprosy. Tokue has lived in a sanatorium since she was afflicted as a young woman, and ventures out in public again shortly before her death to give some meaning to her life.

The fact that there are still several thousand leprosy patients living in sanatoria in Japan shows how close to reality this film is, even today. In Kiyose, where scenes were shot, 200 senior citizens with an average age of 85 are still in this situation.

The compulsory quarantine for leprosy patients introduced in 1907 was not repealed until 1996. Only after this date were the sufferers allowed to leave their 'ghettos'. Many of them were already too old to start a new life in freedom. Yet it was proved many years earlier that the illness – which is called Hansen-Byo (Hansen's disease) in Japan, after the man who discovered it, Norwegian doctor Gerhard Armauer Hansen – could be healed by antibiotics. Forcible castrations and abortions were nevertheless still carried out, and the afflicted were subjected to discrimination and stigmatisation in Japanese society.

In 2001 the Japanese parliament made a public apology to leprosy sufferers and made high compensation payments. The perfectly equipped museum that was opened in 2007 on the subject of leprosy is an indication that the responsible authorities must have had an extremely bad conscience. This place of memorial is situated on the grounds of the sanatorium in Kiyose. Photographs, films and a large number of exhibits illustrate the life of leprosy patients. A brochure printed in English summarises the most important information on the subject.

Some of the books displayed in the library, among which are elaborately designed volumes of photographs, are available free of charge for those who are proficient in Japanese.

Address 国立ハンセン病資料館, The National Hansen's Disease Museum, Aoba-cho 4-1-13, Higashi-Murayama-shi, 189 – 0002 Tokyo, www.hansen-dis.jp/english | Getting there Seibu-Ikebukuro Line (local) to Kiyose, then bus towards Higashi-Murayama to Hansen-Byo-Shiryokan | Hours Tue – Sun 9.30am – 4.30pm*, last admission 4pm, free admission | Tip Tama-Zenshoen Park on the site of the sanatorium is the place where the above-mentioned film was shot.

50___ The Life Safety Learning Center

Don't put it off till tomorrow

No fewer than four continental tectonic plates that collide deep beneath the earth's surface keep Japan in constant movement. Tourists should be aware of the danger that a severe earthquake could hit the centre of Tokyo at any time. The better prepared you are for a possible emergency, the greater chance you will have of saving your own life and the lives of others.

The Life Safety Learning Center of the Ikebukuro fire department familiarises you with this serious subject in an entertaining way. The instructions are given in Japanese, but the films can also be shown in English. At the end of the 90-minute course you will have learned how to operate a fire extinguisher and a great deal about the dangers associated with a heavy earthquake. While you watch the first film, you will be surprised yourself by the outbreak of an earthquake – generated by a simulator, and with a magnitude of between 6 and 7 on the Richter scale. A quake is perceptible from level 4 upwards. The event on 11 March, 2011 reached a maximum intensity of 7 at its epicentre, and a magnitude of 9. This made it the most severe earthquake ever recorded in Japan. At the end of the information and training course you are given tips about how damage, and above all the risk of injury, can be minimised in the home. The courses take place three times daily, and the organisers request advance booking by phone.

In early September, on the anniversary of the great Kanto quake of 1923, disaster protection exercises are held all over the country. If you live in Japan, take advantage of these events! Information and preparation on this serious topic help to reduce fear, and fear is not the best companion if the worst comes to the worst. According to a Japanese saying, 'The catastrophe takes place when you have forgotten about it.' But that doesn't have to happen.

Address 池袋防災館, Ikebukuro Life Safety Learning Center, Nishi-Ikebukuro 2-37-8, Toshima-ku, 171–0021 Tokyo, +81 (0) 335 906 565, www.tfd.metro.tokyo.jp/hp-ikbskan | **Getting there** JR-Yamanote Line and others to Ikebukuro, south or west exit, 5-minute walk | **Hours** Wed–Mon 9am–5pm* (last admission 4.15pm), closed every third Thursday in the month, free admission | **Tip** In Ikebukuro there are many good, cheap Chinese restaurants. Jufukuro is recommended.

51__ The Lighthouse

Fishermen, samurai, convicts and shipbuilders

In 1989 a replica of the old Ishikawajima lighthouse dating from 1866 was completed at the north end of Tsukishima in Tsukuda Park. Surrounded by huge apartment blocks up to 40 storeys high, this tower, tiny in comparison, is a reminder of both the modernisation of Japan in the nineteenth century and of the history of this area, which goes back 400 years.

At that time, when the new seat of government, Edo, was being planned, land reclamation took place in the estuary of the river Sumida. Two sandbanks were turned into the adjacent islands of Ishikawajima and Tsukudajima. One of these was given to the samurai Hachizaemon Ishikawa, who was commander of the shogunate's fleet in the early seventeenth century, and the island was named after him. As time passed, a prison for samurai who had been convicted of crimes was built on the island, as was the first Japanese shipyard working to modern Western standards, a good 100 years later in 1893.

Fishermen from Osaka who had assisted Ieyasu, later the first Edo shogun, settled on neighbouring Tsukudajima, strictly separated from the samurai both socially and in terms of location. He thanked them with a grant of land and fishing grounds with a plentiful yield in the Bay of Edo, thus ensuring them a monopoly of fish supplies for the court and the city of Edo.

However, the move from the Edo to the Tokyo era changed everything: the islands merged thanks to new land reclamation to form the Tsukishima district. The prison and the fisheries moved to new locations in Tokyo, and the shipyard closed in 1979. As the lighthouse no longer lay directly on the bay, it lost its purpose and fell into decay. Its resurrection now sheds light again on the history of the islands, though with unintended irony: the foundations, the only remaining original part of the building, house the park toilets.

Address 石川島灯台, Ishikawa-Lightfire, Tsukuda 1-11, Chuo-ku, 104–0051 Tokyo | Getting there Oedo or Yurakucho metro lines to Tsukishima, 10-minute walk | Tip Right next to the lighthouse, a bridge leads to the remains of the Tsukuda fishing village and the Sumiyoshi Shrine, affiliated to the main shrine that the fishermen brought with them from Osaka.

52_ The Live Bar
School of rock, pop & folk

When the karaoke wave rolled across the world, if not before then, the fact that many Japanese love to sing became well known. But what do people do when they not only sing but also play an instrument, perhaps in a band and want to show off their skills to others? In Japan they go to a so-called live house, or to the smaller version of this, a live bar. They can hire the stage there for a fixed period of time, inviting friends and relatives to come along and listen.

One such live bar, named after a Beatles album, is Rubber Soul in Kokubunji, which was opened in 2002 by three brothers from the Miyadera family, Chisato, Ryo and Takeshi. The name of the bar is not the only reference to the 'fab four'. Alongside an impressive collection of guitars and amplifiers, Beatles memorabilia decorate the walls. Moreover, once a month, on Beatles day, bands who book a slot in advance can perform without paying, provided they play Beatles songs. Similarly, on open-mic day twice a month, all those who put their name on the list can perform free of charge for ten minutes. Furthermore, the owners Ryo and Takeshi sing and play the guitar, while the eldest brother, Chisato is the percussionist. A lively music community has grown up around the bar. From Okinawan music and folk to pop and rock, guests are treated to a wide range of musical styles.

On evenings when no concerts are scheduled, if you don't want to perform yourself, the best thing to do is to take a seat at the bar and watch some music videos or recordings of old concerts. An endless video loop is played, presenting both well-known and almost forgotten music, ranging from the 1950s to the 1980s, in random order. This is guaranteed to make you feel nostalgic. If you get hungry, Rubber Soul serves fish & chips and similar dishes, as well as extremely tasty dry curry and bibimbab in a hot earthenware pot.

Address ラバーソウル, Rubber Soul, Daini-Fuji-Biru B 1, Minamicho 2-16-14, Kokubunji-shi, 185–0021 Tokyo, www.rubber-soul.jp | Getting there JR-Chuo Line and others to Kokubunji, 3-minute walk | Hours Tue–Sun 6pm–midnight, free admission (bar & concert) | Tip Choto, one minute's walk southwest of Kokubunji train station, is a cosy little yakitori restaurant where everything that is edible from a chicken is deliciously grilled on skewers.

53___The Looking-Back Willow
Japan's saddest tree

The place in Taito District that was once called Yoshiwara, a notorious courtesans' quarter during the Edo period, is now a busy road. All traces of the past seem to have been eradicated here. Yet one survival from the old days has been preserved: an old, tomb-like slab of slate on which stand the words 'mikaeri-yanagi', meaning 'looking-back willow'. Above this hangs a sign explaining the story of the tree to which the memorial stone is dedicated.

When guests in the red-light district left the brothels after hours of pleasure, it is said that they would stand for a moment on this spot, where a willow tree stood, and cast a last, wistful glance back at Yoshiwara.

A willow stands here today, but it is not the original one. The trees that previously stood here did not survive catastrophes such as the great Kanto earthquake of 1923 and the Second World War, so new ones have been successively planted in their place. The latest tree is growing in front of a huge petrol station. It has been placed much too close to a mast supporting power lines and its branches are entwined with the cables. This is a troubling sight. Nevertheless, the cult of the tree of sadness is still alive. One reason for this is that it has been mentioned in a number of literary works, most recently in the manga *Tomorrow's Joe*.

Along with the name of the bus stop, which has not been changed, and a post that marks the entrance to the vanished red-light district, the willow is one of the last remaining symbols of the quarter and its history.

If you associate the former district of courtesans with the striking depictions of famous ukiyoe masters and would like to preserve this impression, it is better not to pay a visit today to the district that was once Yoshiwara. The original looking-back willow print, by Hiroshige Utagawa, is exhibited in the Musée Guimet in Paris.

Address 見返り柳, Looking-back Willow, Senzoku 4-10-8, Taito-ku, 111–0031 Tokyo | **Getting there** Hibiya metro line to Minowa, 10-minute walk | **Tip** 8-minute walk from the willow is the Otori Shrine, where the Tori-no-Ichi festival began and huge okame masks can be admired.

54_ The Lowest Tunnel
Watch your head!

Between Shinagawa and Tamachi stations lies Takanawa-kyo-Kado-kyo, which literally means 'the bridge over the Takanawa bridges'. But here you should lay aside your conceptions of what a bridge is: while trains on the Yamanote circular route, many other lines and the Shinkansen thunder above your head at ground level, you will descend to a narrow, single-track tunnel and will have to walk with your head stooped in several places.

This underpass is 230 metres long, and its height at the lowest point is no more than 1.64 metres. For vehicles, the maximum height is restricted to 1.5 metres. This lends a strange, slightly scary atmosphere to the spot. There are noise maniacs who enjoy the infernal sound of trains crashing along above them and like to record their experiences on the Internet. Urban legends on the web report that ghosts have been seen here.

It is recommended to begin the tour on the west side of the tunnel. If you do this, you can gradually get used to the confined conditions. The entrance, relatively inconspicuous, winds down into the ground to the west of a six-lane road. Signs placed there for the benefit of cyclists advise them to dismount and push their bikes. Nevertheless, many of them duck down to the handlebars and whizz through the passage. At first you can walk upright without much difficulty, depending on your height, but the closer you get to the east side, the lower the roof, until finally you can only make progress by bending forward.

As you proceed in the half-light, you will probably notice that a great number of taxis speed past. This subway is one of the few options for them if they want to reach the east side of the Shinagawa train station. For taxis operating in and around Shinagawa a special regulation on height applies so that they don't lose the sign on their roofs when driving through the tunnel.

Address 高輪橋架道橋, Takanawa-kyo-Kado-kyo, Takanawa 2-19-13, Minato-ku, 108–0074 Tokyo | Getting there Asakusa metro line to Sengakuji, exit A 4, 3-minute walk | Tip On the way from the station to the west side of the underpass you pass the ruins of one of the great city gates of Edo, erected here in 1710.

55__The Luxury WC

A privy with a million-dollar atmosphere

If a competition were held for the city with the best public toilets, Tokyo would certainly come out on top. It is never far to the next WC. They are almost always clean, and it costs nothing to use them. It is not unusual for the washrooms of large department stores and restaurants to be fitted with marble cladding or high-quality wood panelling.

The toilet with the most original character in the city is probably the one at Meguro-Gajoen. This complex was built in 1935 as a luxury hotel. Since then, its range of services has been extended: facilities for holding top-class wedding banquets and a wide range of eating and drinking establishments have been added. It is well worth visiting the 'palace of the Shōwa era', as Meguro-Gajoen is popularly called, to have a look around. You will be amazed at the unique interior. In every room the walls and ceilings are decorated with traditional paintings of female beauties. Alongside sumptuous colours, large quantities of gold leaf and black lacquer were used for the picture frames. Roofs covered with tiles, columns, red tori and sculptures complete the overall impression of perfection. The founder's idea was that every guest should be able to feel like a millionaire once in his or her life. Some may find this magnificence over the top, even kitschy – make up your own mind.

The toilets were fitted out in accordance with the extravagant style of the house. To reach them you pass a small garden. The doors are painted in vermilion lacquer and decorated with an intricate mother-of-pearl pattern. Inside, the toilets are spacious with elaborate adornments. In the meantime, modern toilets with seats have replaced those designed for use in a squatting position. To allow the guests to put a pleasant end to a glittering banquet, the washrooms were refurbished in 1991. The costs for this are said to have been more than 85 billion yen.

Address 目黒雅叙園, Meguro-Gajoen, Shimo-Meguro 1-8-1, Meguro-ku, 153 – 0064 Tokyo, www.megurogajoen.co.jp/english | **Getting there** JR-Yamanote Line and others to Meguro, west exit, 4-minute walk | **Tip** Among more than seven restaurants at Gajoen, we recommend the Pandora café-lounge, as it has a view of a wonderful Japanese garden.

56 Manhole Covers
Art beneath your feet

In Japan you come across art in places where you least expect it. Even manhole covers are decorated with imaginative pictures in some places. They are popular surfaces for advertising, praising the merits of tourist attractions, sports clubs and much more. To give variety to these round or rectangular metal slabs, genuine rivalry has broken out between the local authorities that are responsible for the design. The covers for drains or water supply shafts, made entirely from cast iron, are adorned with elaborate patterns and images with true-to-life details. Often they are colourfully painted. To prevent passers-by from slipping when they are wet, the surfaces are not smooth but have clear contours.

Traditional manhole covers often caused people to stumble, so plans were made to replace old models with safer standardised versions. However, in response a community of fans for manhole covers formed, and the proposals had to be withdrawn. Housewives, especially, hunt down the most attractive motifs all over Japan. On the Internet and in books they display photos of their trophies (enter 'manhole' in a search engine). Since 2014 an annual manhole summit has been organised in Tokyo, at which people employed in this business give talks. A competition is held to find the most beautiful manhole cover in the land, and souvenirs such as key rings, ashtrays and beer mats bearing the most popular motifs are on sale.

To see two particularly interesting examples, go to Koganei. On one, a hydrant cover, a fireman in traditional clothing can be seen. In his right hand he holds a matoi, the banner of firefighters, and with his left hand he is waving. A few streets further you can find a drain cover adorned with the motif of a cherry tree in blossom. The next time you take a walk through the streets of Tokyo, don't forget to look down from time to time. It is worthwhile.

Address Nakacho 3-19, Koganei-shi, 184−0012 Tokyo | Getting there JR-Chuo Line (local) to Musashi-Koganei | Tip A 5-minute bus ride from the train station takes you to the Edo-Tokyo Open Air Architectural Museum. Buildings with historic value have been dismantled and rebuilt there.

57__The Measuring Point

From a vital emergency warning station to scrap metal

Tokyo has an ambiguous relationship to water – it is destructive and constructive at one and the same time. On the one hand, there have been serious floods in Tokyo time and again as a result of high tides and typhoons. The damage to infrastructure and property, and also the number of deaths, was enormously high. The particularly tragic flood catastrophe of August 1910 cost more than 1,000 lives and destroyed half a million buildings. To reduce the risk for the future, preventative measures were taken after this disaster. Rivers were divided and dykes were built. This was one reason that the appearance of the city was changed forever. On the other hand, Tokyo Bay holds many possibilities. One important opportunity that it offers is to expand the city by claiming land from the sea to meet the needs of a rapidly growing population.

Since 1873, regular measurements of the water level have been made in the estuary of the river Sumida. If Tokyo Bay presented a threat to the city, this measuring station provided the first indication.

In 1994 a small tower was constructed on the same site and the measuring station moved in there. This structure is called Reiganjima-Suiikansokusho (the water level monitoring point of Reiganjima). Due to its abstract geometric form, the tower seems like an alien element in its surroundings. A twelve-sided steel polygon at the centre of which is the deck for monitoring. Wrapped around it is an iron catwalk, from which a walkway connects to dry land. Measurements are still taken here.

However, the site of the main station for monitoring the water level was moved a few years ago to Aburatsubo in Kanagawa. The reason for this is a change in the water level caused by precipitation and other influences. This means that the observation point in the river Sumida has little more than symbolic significance today.

Address 霊岸島水位観測所, Reiganjima Water Level Observatory, Shinkawa 2-32, Chuo-ku, 104–0033 Tokyo | **Getting there** Hibiya metro line to Hatchobori, exit B 3, 8-minute walk | **Tip** One metro stop away, close to Kayaba-cho station, is the base of Great Cycling Tours, where you can book an organised bike trip through the city.

58__Modern Coin-Op Cleaning
My beautiful launderette

Are coin-operated laundries (coin-randorii) obsolete? Not in Japan. Their numbers have doubled nationwide in the last ten years. The reasons for this boom are obvious: modern coin-operated launderettes offer much the same as laundries with service, but at a much lower cost, and customers need not wait long to pick up their washing. Larger items that don't fit in the home washing machine, such as woollen blankets and futons, are freed from dust and house mites by a wash. The dryer, which operates at a temperature of approximately 70 degrees Celsius, has the advantage of freeing clothes from pollen during the hay fever season. Ingrained dirt that clings to sports shoes disappears in shoe-washing machines as if by magic. Many launderettes are fitted out to be cosy places. To make the wait seem shorter for customers, they often have a manga library or a television. So that no one has to hang around for a long time waiting for a machine to be available, the Clean Best chain offers its Realtime-Service. Before setting off for the launderette, customers can check on the homepage how many machines are occupied at that moment. If they are registered at their local branch, they receive a customer card and can be informed by e-mail when the washing cycle is at an end.

The branch of Clean Best in Kitazawa is extremely proud of an innovative washing machine that features an aqua-clean system. It employs a special new technology for the last rinse. Electrolytic water is used for this rinse. This method of cleaning clothes has a low environmental impact, as no chemicals are added to the water. Even laundry that is extremely dirty comes out clean without any difficulties thanks to this process.

If a friendly member of staff is not available when you arrive, you will find instructions for operating all the machines at the laundry.

Address クリーンベストチェーン, Clean Best chain, Kitazawa 5-19-13, Setagaya-ku, 155−0031 Tokyo, www.sanyo-clean-best.com (only in Japanese) | **Getting there** Keio-New Line (local) to Sasazuka, 8-minute walk | **Hours** Daily 6am–1am | **Tip** A 15-minute walk takes you to the fashionable Shimo-Kitazawa quarter. Here an antique shop called Antiquaille sells porcelain and glass from the Meiji era onwards.

59__ The Monorail

Almost like a roller coaster, though no loops

Since 1964 the Tokyo Monorail has been running between Haneda Airport and Hamamatsucho Station. Commercially it is one of the world's most successful transport links of its kind. Originally intended only as a connection to the airport for the Tokyo Olympic Games in 1964, it later got six more stations between the two terminals, and there are plans to extend the line – as originally conceived – to Shinbashi and Tokyo's main train station.

It is a standing single-rail system. This means that, in addition to the rubber wheels that run along the rail, there are further rubber wheels on either side of the rail to keep the train on its track. What seemed like futuristic technology for long distances in the immediate post-war period soon proved to be too expensive in many parts of the world, and in the end monorails were only used for short journeys.

In the case of the Tokyo Monorail, the advantages of this mode of transport are fully exploited: as only one rail is necessary, less space is required than for conventional rail systems and it is possible to take much tighter bends. In order to avoid purchasing a lot of land, much of the monorail passes above water. In accordance with this, the route was adapted to the course of the waterways with a lot of curves.

If your purpose is not merely to reach the airport as quickly as possible, take the slow, 20-minute connection in the local train and try to get a seat at the very front or back of the carriage. The bench seats parallel to the side windows are recommended, as they provide a perfect panoramic view of Tokyo Bay. When you have sat down, the monorail literally rumbles off, in places at a rapid speed of up to 80 kilometres per hour, and leans into the bends. And so you rush to your destination, above and below bridges and through tunnels, almost as if you were on a roller coaster.

Address 東京モノレール, Tokyo Monorail, Hamamatsucho 2-4-12, Minato-ku, 105–0013 Tokyo, www.tokyo-monorail.co.jp/english/guide/line/index.html | Getting there JR-Yamanote Line and others to Hamamatsucho | Hours Daily 4.58–12.01am, every five minutes | Tip You get a fine view of Tokyo Bay from the observation platform of the inland terminal. In good weather you can see the other side of the bay, as planes climb steeply into the sky in front of you.

60__The Monshuin Temple

Zazen refreshes the mind and cleanses the spirit

This tip is completely unsuitable for late risers. On Sundays at 5.30am a group meets for a zazen session at the Monshuin Temple in Ome. To set the mood, green tea is served in the cosy common room. Sitting on tatami mats, the participants gradually strike up conversation. Those who are still too tired can simply doze or enjoy the morning atmosphere in silence.

The session starts at 6.10am on the dot. Everyone goes to the main hall of the temple and takes a zafu, a special meditation cushion, which is laid on a zabuton, a seat cushion, and finds a place. As participants are not supposed to change their sitting position in the following 40 minutes, it is important to take up a posture that is as comfortable as possible. Then the meditation begins. Even if you cannot understand the words of the monk Masaya Tanaka, the timbre of his voice has a calming effect, and you will start to relax after a short time.

From outside, the temple does not present a striking appearance. Inside, however, it is decorated with beautiful woodcarvings, and worth a visit for that reason. In addition to the weekly zazen group, the Monshuin Temple puts on regular concerts. In Golden Week in May a three-day intensive zazen workshop is held.

There is also the option of booking a private zazen meditation. One group that regularly takes advantage of this consists of senior citizens. They call themselves the teinen-juku, the school of pensioners. Following the meditation, the 14 members talk in small groups, speaking with astonishing openness about their marital problems. As the leader of the group, Sayako Nishida, puts it: 'The dankai-sedai (the generation of baby boomers born after the Second World War) did not learn how to talk about such things. In this respect, the zazen session works wonders. It frees the mind and cleanses the spirit!' She recommends zazen for everybody.

Address 聞修院, Monshuin Temple, Kurosawa 3-1578, Ome-shi, 198−0005 Tokyo, +81 (0) 428 745 411, www.monsyuin.org (only in Japanese) | Getting there JR-Chuo Line to Ome, 40-minute walk | Hours Daily 9am−4pm; it is not necessary to book a zazen session, but advisable to phone before going, as sessions can be cancelled. | Tip For a walk from the temple, take a 45-minute stroll to Ome Tetsudo Park, a railway park with old steam locomotives.

61___ The Mound Grave

Burial site of one of the first residents of Tokyo

Since the seventh century, long before Edo and later Tokyo become the seat of government for Japan, this province was called Musashi. Musashi-no-Kuni, which literally means Musashino Country, covered a great deal of the area that is now Tokyo, Kanagawa and Saitama. The city of Fuchu, today to the west of Tokyo, was the seat of the provincial government, which is exactly what Fuchu means: provincial administration.

In addition to government buildings and temples, the area was densely dotted with the graves of leading government servants. Over the centuries, these kofun ('old graves'), as such sites are called, became overgrown and eventually resembled small hills. One of these tombs, close to the Nishifu train station right next to the Kumano Shrine, was excavated at the beginning of this century. The structure, which had partly collapsed, was reconstructed.

As a result, today it is possible to admire once again this large structure, which measures approximately 30 by 30 metres and has three stages: on the square base there stands a second section, also square in plan, and on this in turn a circular third stage. The two upper sections are lined with round stones that were brought here from the nearby river Tama. On the side facing the shrine is an entrance, closed with big stone slabs.

In a museum that seems extremely oversized in relation to the number of exhibits, details of the excavation and reconstruction of the kofun are presented. Visitors can also put on a helmet and take a flashlight to enter a replica of the tomb chamber. One of the main attractions, in a glass case in the middle of the room, is a facsimile of one of the few items found in the grave: a small decorated sword tip. When it was opened, a few glass beads and nails were found, but neither a body nor a coffin. Earlier 'visitors' had taken them as a souvenir.

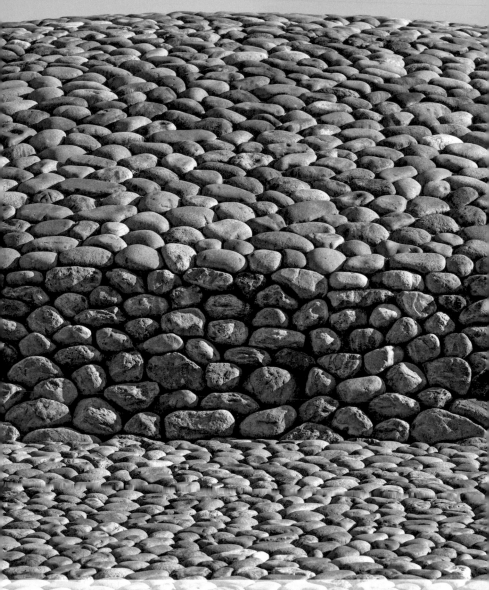

Address 武蔵府中熊野神社古墳, Musashino-Fuchu-Kumano-Jinja-Kofun, Nishifu-cho 2-9-5, Fuchu-shi, 183–0031 Tokyo | Getting there JR-Nanbu Line to Nishifu, 7-minute walk | Hours Museum Tue–Sun 9am–5pm*, free admission | Tip On the other side of the Nishifu train station you can get an impression of the appearance of the kofun before reconstruction: a further grave mound in a park there is still covered with earth and overgrown by trees.

62__The New Otaku Paradise
Still a tip for insiders

Akihabara is still regarded as the Mecca of the otaku (nerds), but insiders already know that the golden days of this world-famous nerd zone are numbered. In another place, a paradise for otaku with a new dimension is emerging. A few minutes' walk from Nakano train station is Nakano Broadway, a seemingly normal shopping centre. Yet if you take a closer look, you will be astonished. More than 100 hobby shops have come together at this address, and their number is increasing. At Nakano Broadway fans find everything that has made Japanese pop culture famous: manga, anime, computer games, consoles, CDs, figures, collectors' cars, and so on and so forth.

The well-known manga chain Mandarake has opened a megastore on three floors. Here the shelves fill the whole space between the floor and the ceiling, and are brimming over with second-hand mangas. The prices start at 100 yen, and the sky is the limit. For a hand-signed scene from Hayao Miyazaki's *My Neighbour Totoro*, passionate collectors can expect to fork out several million yen.

At Anime World Star celluloid prints, called cels for short, are on sale. You can choose between popular scenes and complete anime series of well-loved works on these prints. Tokyo-Maker is a unique copy shop. It was the very first store in Japan that offered a 3-D print service. At Robot-Robot you can purchase robots in every conceivable shape and size. Godzilla and Ultraman are included in the product range. Or how about a T-shirt with an amusing Japanese slogan printed on the front? You will find a large assortment of so-called baka shirts (stupid shirts) at I-ire.

The enormous range of items offered at this hotspot for otaku may seem overwhelming to the uninitiated trying to get their bearings. However, it does convey a vague impression of what fans find so fascinating about their passion.

Address 中野ブロードウェイ, Nakano-Broadway, Nakano 5-52-15, Nakano-ku, 164−0001 Tokyo, www.nbw.jp/#!/en | **Getting there** JR-Chuo Line to Nakano | **Hours** Please see the website, as the shops have individual opening times. | **Tip** Daily Chico on the ground floor of Nakano Broadway sells tokudai soft ice-cream − huge, piled-up portions in many different flavours.

63__ The New Yokocho
A culinary strip with regional cuisine

Down-at-heel bars and pubs mark the lanes. Red lanterns hang in front of them, but the colour faded long ago. The signs are old-fashioned, the posters weathered and peeling. These are the dominant features of the urban scene around the lanes known as yokocho. This shabby exterior conceals an entirely different world on the inside. In Izakaya, a crowded place in the evening, the mood is cheerful and relaxed. Off-key sounds waft out to the street from a karaoke bar, and the smoke emerging from the yakitori bars stings the eyes. The atmosphere is a little bit disreputable and sleazy. There is no sign of sterile tidiness around here.

Since 2010 there has been a yokocho with an innovative concept. Yurakucho Sanchoku Inshokugai, partly beneath the platforms of Yurakucho station, is a food alley where specialities from rural regions of Japan are served. The fresh ingredients are supplied to the restaurants by farmers and fishermen from various prefectures. Diners can choose between dishes from Hokkaido, Iwate, Nagano, Shizuoka and Kumamoto. Those who like to eat fish and meat will find a diverse range of delicious meals. The menus also include some out-of-the-ordinary items like beef tongue and horse meat. The alcoholic drinks on offer in each eatery also come from the region that is showcased there.

Foreign visitors are extremely welcome, and to help them, there are even English-language menus with explanatory photos of the dishes. If onuma steak from Hokkaido takes your fancy, but your companion prefers to eat ramen with gyoza (soup with stuffed noodles), this presents no problem. You can order dishes from different part of the country and eat them together in one place. All of which means that a visit to this yokocho provides more than just a good meal. It is also an unrivalled opportunity to explore Japan's regional culinary variety.

Address 有楽町産直飲食街, Yurakucho Sanchoku Inshokugai, Yurakucho 2-1-1, Chiyodaku, 100–0006 Tokyo | **Getting there** Ginza metro line and others to Yurakucho, exit C1, 5-minute walk | **Tip** The restaurants Ton-Ton and Kinryo in the railway arches have been in business since the 1950s serving yakitori, fried chicken skewers. The atmosphere is – different, shall we say?

64_ The Nihonbashi Cruise
Down by the waterline

In the days when it was still called Edo, Tokyo was one of the world's largest cities with a population of one million. This caused considerable logistical problems. As progress was slow and laborious on its narrow streets, the principal arteries for transport were the rivers.

These waterways had little in common with natural rivers, as their courses were radically adapted to meet the requirements of urban planning. Apart from two very wide rivers, the Sumida and the Arakawa, waterways are not much in evidence in the appearance of the city today, as rivers and streams flow in the shadow of elevated roads and have been either confined to channels of concrete or completely covered up.

A good starting point for exploring these historic highways is the Nihonbashi Bridge. There has been a small pier for shops at the foot of the bridge, at its southeastern end, since 2011. From here, uncovered boats take those who are interested on tours that allow a view of Tokyo with a difference. Two tours (45 and 60 minutes) on the river Nihonbashi head towards Sumida and return to the starting point along the river Kameshima. The longer trip makes a detour out into Tokyo Bay. The 90-minute tour on the river Kanda starts off by heading in the opposite direction, inland, on the Nihonbashi and then the Kanda, returning to Nihonbashi via the river Sumida.

Especially when taking the boat on the Sumida and to Tokyo Bay, you will notice that industrial areas have been transformed into extremely upmarket residential and business districts. Where once there were only industrial buildings, warehouses and plain residential buildings, now more and more apartment high-rises are shooting up. You should also keep an eye open for the numerous handsome bridges, many of them very old, beneath which your boat passes from time to time.

Address 日本橋クルーズ, Nihonbashi-Cruise, Nihonbashi 1-9, Chuo-ku, 103–0027 Tokyo, www.ss3.jp/nihonbashi-cruise | Getting there Ginza metro line and others to Nihonbashi | Hours As departure times depend on the weather, consult the timetable on Twitter (@TokyoBay_Cruise). | Tip Nearby you can go to COREDO-Muromachi, a modern shopping centre that aims for a contemporary take on the atmosphere of old Nihonbashi in the Edo period.

65__The Ninja Clan
Mrs Shibata's family secret

Many fans of Japan discovered their love of the country from Hollywood productions such as *Shogun* and *The Last Samurai*. These cliché-ridden films arouse longings for a world of brave samurai that never existed in the way it is portrayed. In this world the ninja, secret warriors with special martial arts skills, have a special appeal for many people with Japan nostalgia.

For first-hand information on these subjects, go to the Musashi Ninja Clan in Tabata. Its founder, Mrs Shibata, comes from a samurai family and numbers ninja among her ancestors. For a long time she knew nothing of this legacy until one day her father, a swordsmith, revealed the secret at last.

But even before Mrs Shibata heard about the family history, she was interested in ninja. For many years she worked as a tourist guide, and began to organise demonstrations on this subject for children and adults, because little was available in this field for foreign tourists.

One day, when her ninja master handed in his notice after accepting an offer of employment at the imperial court, her father came to her aid. He introduced his ninja pupils to his daughter and took the opportunity to reveal the family secret. He had promised her grandfather that he would not tell his daughter until 50 years after the old man's death: the grandfather was ashamed of the fact that he had been a hired killer. For this reason he later converted to Christianity and served in the Salvation Army.

The ninja school occupies premises in an old two-storey building. On the upper floor there is an exhibition space where old ninja tools are on display. On the ground floor is the dojo, where ninja shows, workshops and screenings of films are regularly held. Here, in the house of Mrs Shibata, you will experience an entertaining introduction to Japanese history.

外国奉行 柴田剛中

文久遣欧使節組頭

Address 時代アカデミー道場, Musashi Ninja Clan, Tabata 6-3-5, Kita-ku, 114–0014 Tokyo, +81 (0) 903 691 8165, office@musashi.ninja, www.musashi.ninja | **Getting there** JR-Yamanote Line to Tabata, 4-minute walk | **Hours** By arrangement; book two weeks in advance, if possible | **Tip** In the Tabata Memorial Museum of Writers and Artists near the station you can learn about several well-known authors who came from this area.

66_ The Oizumi Anime Gate

Where Astro-Boy learned to walk

The cradle of Japanese anime is Nerima. The first animated colour film was made here in 1958. It was *The Tale of the White Serpent* (*Hakujaden*), based on an original Chinese version and produced by the Toei Anime Studios.

The legendary manga artist Osamu Tezuka founded the studio Mushi-Production as a competitor to Toei. Here the first anime for Japanese television was created, based on his Astro-Boy manga series. In 1963 the 193 episodes of the series, each lasting 25 minutes, were broadcast on the Fuji TV channel. This was followed by further successful films.

Today animes are a lucrative business sector, and Nerima is still the Mecca of the industry. Some 80 companies are associated with the production of animated films there. In honour of the birthplace of Japanese animation, various attractions have been created. One of these is the Oizumi Anime Gate at the north exit of Higashi-Oizumi-Gakuen train station. It was inaugurated in April 2015. Two gates as tall as a man were installed outside the station and perforated in a pattern to make them look like strips of unexposed film. Life-sized golden statues of well-known characters were set up around the square. You will see the superstar Astro-Boy, and a little further the mysterious Maetel and Tetsuro Hoshino, the boy from the slums, both from Reiji Matsumoto's *Galaxy Express 999*. The orphan Joe Yabuki, who became a boxer (*Tomorrow's Joe* by Tetsuya Chiba) and the alien girl Princess Lum (*Urusei Yatsura* by Rumiko Takahashi) have been commemorated there.

A chronology presents the most important works from the genre and uses photographs to show how it has changed over the last 60 years. These highlight attractions and frequent events draw fans from far and near to Nerima, a place that in other respects only has a reputation as a dormitory town.

Address 大泉アニメゲート, Oizumi-Anime-Gate, Higashi-Oizumi 5–41, Nerima-ku, 178–0063 Tokyo, www.animation-nerima.jp/nerima-and-animation/animegate | Getting there Seibu-Ikebukuro Line (local) to Higashi-Oizumi-Gakuen | Tip In the entire area around Nerima you encounter anime characters, for example a street light in the shopping arcade on the north side of Oizumi-Gakuen station decorated with a motif from Reiji Matsumoto's *Galaxy Express 999*.

67 ___ The Old Bathhouse
Body care in charming historical surroundings

Until the middle of the last century, no Japanese home had a bath – fire prevention regulations prohibited the heating of water on an open fire. This is why people went to a sento, a public bathhouse, to wash. Today a sento is more of a social institution, a meeting place and also a welcome, stylish, generously sized alternative to the tiny bathtubs that are installed in urban apartments.

One bathhouse that has preserved its original charm is Fuji-no-Yu in Nerima. It is a unique survival from the post-war period, and the trip is a rewarding experience from the very moment you arrive at the Shakujii-koen train station, from where you reach the wonderfully old-fashioned bath after a 15-minute walk through a maze of narrow lanes.

The traditional bathhouse building with its gabled roof creates the impression that you might have arrived at an old mansion. You enter through a wooden door, with decoration of stone reliefs on each side. A huge number of shoe compartments in the lobby gives an idea of the bustling activity that must have characterised Fuji-no-Yu in times past. Today things are more relaxed. The admission price is 460 yen, and guests are advised to bring their own towels, though it is possible to hire them for a charge. The wet zone is divided according to gender. The two sides of the bathhouse have an identical, mirror-symmetrical layout beneath a single roof. The space is divided down the middle by a wall about two and a half metres high, and is reminiscent of an old gymnasium. In each part there are two baths with water at different temperatures. Tiles with a weeping-willow motif adorn the back wall.

In spite of all the symmetry, the men's bath has one advantage compared to the women's bath: it has a glass wall, beyond which is an aquarium with koi carp. According to an old rule, to this day women are not permitted to see the fish.

Address 富士の湯, Fuji-no-Yu, Mihara-Dai 1-30-1, Nerima-ku, 177–0031 Tokyo | **Getting there** Seibu-Ikebukuro Line to Shakujii-koen | **Hours** Tue–Sun 4–11pm | **Tip** Follow the road to the south exit from the station to reach the extensive Shakujii-koen park with its attractive lakes.

68__ The Old Police Station
Friends and helpers from a bygone age

Alongside the large, multistorey police stations in Japan there is a dense network of smaller ones, which are called koban. The word means 'change of shift', a reference to rotation of staffing. They are often situated at train stations and strategically important crossroads, and one or several policemen are on duty there. For this reason, the size of the stations varies: whereas new buildings usually have two storeys and are sometimes built in a strikingly eccentric style, the tiny old ones often accommodate only two police officers.

The purpose of a koban is above all to maintain close contact to the local population in order to prevent crimes or make it possible to intervene quickly. However, stories are also told of over-enthusiastic officers who spied on residents. A further important function, especially in the days before mapping apps on smartphones, was to give directions to people who did not know the locality: a koban has an exact plan of its precinct, showing the way through the complicated labyrinth of addresses. As the smaller koban stations are not always occupied, each has a special intercom system that can be used to sound an emergency alarm or put questions to the local headquarters.

The oldest such police station in Tokyo is the one in Nishinakadori. It was constructed of wood in 1921 and replaced by a concrete structure in 1926. To this day it has kept its external appearance: inside is a tiny antechamber for visitors, and beyond this the officers' room, which is not much bigger. (In the Edo-Tokyo Open Air Architectural Museum in Koganei you can visit the interior of a similar building.)

If you are in luck and the koban is occupied, the officer on duty might even give you some tips about sights in the district, where there are still many old shops, some of them with magnificent façades, an environment that the koban matches well.

Address 西仲通り地域安全センター, Nishinakadori Chiiki Anzen Center, Tsukishima 3-4-3, Chuo-ku, 104–0052 Tokyo | **Getting there** Oedo Line to Tsukishima, exit A7, 5-minute walk | **Tip** The police station is in the middle of Monja Street, where countless little restaurants serve monja-yaki, a Tokyo speciality that you should not miss.

69 __ The Old Post Station

A forerunner of the highway service station

In the Edo period, the journey on foot from Edo, present-day Tokyo, to Kyoto took approximately twelve days by the Tokaido route. For an overnight stay, post stations were available to travellers at regular intervals.

The Tokaido road was Japan's most famous, and train lines are still named after it today, but there were four other roads that linked the seat of government to the provinces. The Koshukaido road, on which the Hino post station lies, led through the mountains west of Tokyo to what is now Yamanashi Prefecture.

The routes to Edo were used by merchants and also by nobles – samurai from the provinces and court aristocrats from Kyoto. These roads made it possible to control the whole country from Edo. For example, in the mid-nineteenth century the shinsengumi, a division of the police, were sent to bring law and order to Kyoto, which was troubled at that time. Several leading members of this police corps came from Hino and passed through the Hino post station.

To provide accommodation that was fitting for nobles, most post stations were strictly divided between a part for the aristocracy and a part for the 'common people'. Whereas the operators of the stations were allowed to take payment from non-noble travellers, they could not take money from aristocrats. In compensation they could occupy the office of mayor of their community, and part of their building served as the town hall. This was the case at Hino-juku.

What remains of the old complex of buildings today is a gate and the main house, dating from the nineteenth century, which was used for various purposes, including the production of noodles. Having survived demolition, it is now home to a museum, where visitors can see the lovely old rooms of the post station and a few display cases with information about its history. Tours of the building in Japanese are held.

Address 日野宿本陣, Hinojuku-Honjin, Hinohonmachi 2-15-9, Hino-shi, 191–0011 Tokyo | Getting there JR-Chuo Line to Hino, 10-minute walk | Hours Tue–Sun 9.30am–5pm* | Tip On the way to the train station you can stop at the playfully chaotic Yumekuraya to eat and buy craftwork.

70__ The One-Coin Restaurant
A culinary passport

Tokyo has an extremely high density of restaurants, said to be much higher than that in, for example, New York. The range of alternative eateries is overwhelming, and the competition between them undoubtedly benefits thrifty customers.

As a means of standing up to the low-cost chains and the fast-food outlets, many restaurants offer a 'one-coin lunch', which costs only 500 yen. For this modest price, diners are served a complete menu with rice, meat or fish and a soup, sometimes including a drink. However, the price may have risen in some establishments a little, perhaps by up to 100 yen.

One izakaya that participates in this promotion is Suzume no Oyado in Ochanomizu, which provides down-to-earth Japanese food. Diners can choose between five different midday menus, and wash down the food with beer on special offer.

As a method of making it easier to find one-coin restaurants, the 'lunch passport' was invented. This is a little booklet that can be purchased in bookshops, and is now available for many Japanese cities. For Tokyo the booklets are organised according to district. A marked plan helps you to find your way around. When arriving at one of the restaurants that are included, you have to present your lunch passport to be entitled to the cut-price menu. Each diner has to present his or her own pass, and gets it stamped for each menu that is ordered. You can take advantage of the offer up to three times, depending on the policy of the individual restaurant. At some of them a limited number of saver menus are served per day, so it is advisable to arrive in good time. Like a normal passport, the booklet has an expiry date. The period of validity varies according to the region. In some areas the lunch passport is for three months, in others for four. And even if you use it only two or three times, the investment of about 1,000 yen pays off.

Address すずめのおやど, Suzume no Oyado, Kanda Surugadai 2-1-29, Chiyoda-ku, 101–0062 Tokyo, +81 (0) 332 912 538 | **Getting there** JR-Chuo Line and others to Ochanomizu | **Hours** Daily 11am–2pm (lunch) | **Tip** Walk up the slope for five minutes to reach the Hilltop Hotel. It was originally the Institute for a New Lifestyle, and was not converted to a hotel until 1954. Famous writers such as Yasunari Kawabata, Yukio Mishima and Shusaku Endo liked to go there.

71 __ The Owl Café
Tu-whit tu-whoo

Pet cafés where dogs or cats can be stroked are not uncommon in Japan. In recent years, however, more and more kinds of animals, some of them exotic, have found their way into teahouses. One of these is the owl, which can otherwise only be seen in a zoo. As in Europe, the owl is considered to be a wise creature in Japan. The Harry Potter stories aroused interest in these mysterious forest birds, and the result was the opening of several owl cafés in Tokyo since 2012.

One of them is Owl Village in Harajuku. Visitors can not only watch the birds here, but also stroke them and, on request, have them perch on their arms or shoulders. They are also allowed to take photographs, though the flash has to be switched off. The admission fee of 2,500 yen includes one drink, and the visiting time is restricted to an hour.

On entering the café, first of all you are shown to your table, where you are served a drink and, if you would like, a dessert. From here you can watch the birds in their glasshouse in the middle of the room, while enjoying the relaxed atmosphere. After about half an hour, the time has come: a member of the staff will come over and lead you to the world of the owls. Before this happens, a few explanations are given about how to handle the birds in a suitable way. You can also prepare your visit in advance by looking at the Owl Village homepage. An entertaining film demonstrates what kind of behaviour is to be avoided during contact with the birds.

At present, Owl Village has eight owls from a wide variety of species. On request, and for an additional charge, it is possible to feed them. Visitors are allowed to stay in the owl house for 35 minutes. This long period is an advantage of the place in comparison with some of the other owl houses, where customers are only permitted to spend 10 minutes with the birds.

Address フクロウの里, Owl Village, Harajuku-ATM-Bldg. 4F, Jingumae 1-21-15, Shibuya-ku, 150−0001 Tokyo, www.owlvillage.jp/english/harajuku | Getting there JR-Yamanote Line to Harajuku, exit to Takeshita and 1 minute on foot | Hours Daily 11am−7pm | Tip At the start of the street Takeshita-Dori you will find Kimono Tokyo, where you can hire a kimono. Thus traditionally dressed, you can have your photo taken at the Meiji Shrine.

72 __ The Pet Cemetery

A final resting place for Pochi & Tama

The Japanese love animals. The number of pets owned is growing larger and larger, and at the same time the birth rate is declining. For many people, a dog or a cat has become a substitute for children, and so their four-legged darlings are thoroughly spoiled. When Pochi or Tama – these are the commonest names for dogs and cats respectively – pass away, their owners want to pay their last respects in a fitting way. It would not really be a problem to dispose of them with the household rubbish, as under the law, dead pets are classified as 'combustible waste'.

With the boom in pets in the 1990s, the fortunes of animal undertakers began to prosper. There had already been ceremonial burials of animals, but these were performed for those that had been used in experiments and then killed. The purpose was to appease their spirits. Today, in all of Japan, there are more than 900 pet cemeteries, of which 120 are run by Buddhist temples.

These Buddhist pet cemeteries exist for religious reasons. Although it is bad karma to be reborn as an animal, and animals are generally regarded as unclean, according to Buddhist beliefs they have a soul and are capable of suffering. Furthermore, their owners become very fond of them, regarding them as members of the family.

Since 1921 the Jikeiin Temple in Fuchu has maintained one of the best-known animal cemeteries in Tokyo. Various forms of burial are possible here. The cheapest of them is cremation of several deceased pets together, but it is possible to have an individual ceremony at which the owner or family is present. The ashes are then placed in a common or an individual grave, or the owners take an urn home with them.

Depending on their specific wishes, the funeral of a cat costs between 15,000 and 54,000 yen. For dogs the prices are higher, and vary according to the size of the animal.

Address 慈恵院 多摩犬猫霊園, Jikeiin Tama-Inuneko-Reien, Sengen-cho 2-15-1, Fuchu-shi, 183–0001 Tokyo | Getting there Keio Line to Higashi-Fuchu, 20-minute walk or bus 75 to Sengenyama-Koen | Hours Daily 8am–5pm | Tip A little further to the northeast is Tama-Reien, Japan's biggest urban cemetery and one of the country's first park cemeteries. In addition to many famous political and military figures, the writer Yukio Mishima is buried there.

73__The Philosophy Park
Concepts and commemoration

When translating from the Japanese, the question of which words to choose often arises: which version is better, 'Philosophy Park' or, closer to the original and usual in English translation, 'Garden Temple of Philosophy'? A similar dilemma applies to the main building of the sanctuary, which is dedicated to the 'saints' Kant, Socrates, Confucius and Buddha. This is a bewildering description, again based on a translation issue: even if you render 'saint' as 'master', open questions remain.

Similar difficulties must have confronted the Buddhist and philosopher Enryo Inoue: in the Meiji period, when Japan was modernising rapidly, he was a scholar with a public reputation who popularised both Eastern and the brand-new Western ways of thinking. For this purpose, he repeatedly had to find the right Japanese word to express Western concepts – and vice versa.

He disseminated his ideas through his teaching at the university, lecture tours in Japan and abroad, and the philosophy park, which he founded in 1904 as a place of 'spiritual cultivation'. Originally he intended the park to be the seat of a university, but the plans were abandoned, and the institution now called Toyo University was built elsewhere. Today this university still holds events in the park: philosophy lectures and, on the first Saturday in November, the 'philosophy ceremony', which Inoue initiated in 1885.

In the park you will find many buildings, some of them strange-looking, which represent different philosophies: in addition to the above-mentioned Shiseido (Hall of Four Saints), note the Rokkendai (Pagoda of the Six Sages), which commemorates six scholars from Japan, China and India. The paths, too, have meanings, with the intention of conveying spiritual insights to visitors. What does the Keiken-Zaka (Way of Knowledge) stand for? Search for inspiration and philosophise for yourself.

Address 哲学堂公園, Tetsugakudo-Koen, Matsugaoka 1-34-28, Nakano-ku, 165–0024 Tokyo, www.tetsugakudo.jp (Japanese) | Getting there Seibu-Shinjuku Line (local) to Araiyakushi-mae, 10-minute walk | Hours Daily 9am–5pm, with other times for some of the buildings (see website) | Tip Close by, to the southeast of the park, is a magnificent, colourful Buddhist temple, Arai-Yakushi.

74__The Photo Gallery

From East Asia to the whole world

In Tokyo it is difficult to keep up to date about the latest exhibitions, as there are simply too many, and even a website as well organised as TokyoArtBeat does not list everything. This also applies to photography, although this field of fine art did not get its own gallery in Tokyo until 1978, when the Zeit-Foto Salon opened.

The leading address for photographic art for a long time, it has been joined by more and more new locations. One of these is the Zen Foto Gallery, and the German spelling of 'Foto' in its name is a conscious act of homage to the Zeit-Foto Salon. In 2009 Mark Pearson, an English-born photographer and a passionate photographic collector, opened this gallery.

Although Pearson was not a gallerist by profession, his main employment in the finance sector gave him the necessary resources to run the gallery successfully. This is the reason for the 'Zen' in the name: just as Zen stands for the release from ties, the gallery was, at least originally, not tied to other existing institutions.

As Pearson and the gallery manager, Amanda Lo from Taiwan, did not yet have a network, they made a virtue out of necessity, exhibiting the work of young, new photographers from East Asia, usually Japan and China, alongside that of older, forgotten Japanese artists whom the established galleries neglected. This gave the Zen Foto Gallery a unique profile, enabling it to provide an excellent survey of photography in Japan from the pre-war era to the present day.

Books on photography made a big contribution – both exhibition catalogues and electronic versions of classic photo books that were long out of print, produced by the gallery's own online publisher Shashasha. Other publishers can put their books on the Shashasha website, which makes it the most comprehensive catalogue of Japanese photographic publications, with fans all over the world.

Address Zen Foto Gallery, Piramide 2F, Roppongi 6-6-9, Minato-ku, 106–0032 Tokyo, www.zen-foto.jp, www.shashasha.co/en | **Getting there** Oedo Line and others to Roppongi, 4-minute walk | **Hours** Tue–Sat noon–7pm, admission free | **Tip** The Zen Foto Gallery is one of many galleries in the Piramide Building, which is worth a visit. On the ground floor you can drink coffee in the courtyard of Roti or craft beer outside.

75__ The Pigeon's Nest

Almost no people – in Tokyo!

The idea that most people have of Tokyo is an almost endless sea of buildings: asphalt, concrete, glass and steel are the materials of this mega-city, where millions bustle about. But there are different sides to Tokyo, as the prefecture of the capital extends from Tokyo Bay far to the west, to the rural mountain region of Okutama. In a narrow, sparsely populated valley lies the quiet village of Hatonosu, which means 'pigeon's nest'.

The village is divided by the river Tama, which here rushes shallow but not wide through the deep Hatonosu Gorge. From here you can take walking trails along the Tama further into the hinterland, to Lake Okutama or in the opposite direction across a low chain of mountains to the neighbouring village, Kori. It is also worth staying in Okutama for a while on account of its many wild-looking views of the river and the adjoining, densely forested mountains.

To get your bearings, walk from the train station down to the narrow road bridge across the Hatonosu Gorge, from where you can admire a superb panorama. Then go a little way back towards the main road and follow one of the many paths to the riverbank. Rusty walkways, crumbling flights of steps and abandoned buildings exude an air of morbid tranquillity. Hidden on the slope is a metre-high waterfall, which flows unnoticed between the road and the houses.

In the valley you should not fail to climb around and on to the massive rock that blocks your view. If you do this, you will get a worm's-eye view of the narrow, gigantic gorge in front of you. In the valley you will also find a low suspension bridge that opens up further wonderful prospects. As you walk up and down, here and there, in this natural environment, you will hardly realise how quickly time passes. But there is one thing that you are sure to notice: here you will seldom or never encounter other people.

Address 鳩ノ巣, Hatonosu, Okutama-machi Tanazawa 390, Nishitama-gun, 198–0106 Tokyo | Getting there JR-Ome Line to Hatonosu | Tip Go to the Popo Café at the foot of the suspension bridge to enjoy dishes made with local vegetables while you look out at the gorge from the panorama window.

76_ The Pink Taxi

Just once: feel like a celebrity

A trip in a taxi is truly an experience in Japan. As the fight for survival in the market is extremely tough, Tokyo's taxi firms have come up with a lot of ideas to differentiate themselves from competitors. There are women's taxis with female drivers, luxurious limousines for longer journeys and so-called turtle taxis, in which passengers can press a button as a signal that they would like to be driven very slowly. There seem to be no limits to the inventiveness of the taxi operators. And whichever taxi you choose, there is no extra charge for luxury, and the drivers do not expect to receive tips.

A recent addition to this diversity appeared on the streets of the capital in late 2013: a brightly coloured taxi that catches the eye among all the black cabs. The Pink Crown Taxi was produced by Toyota in that year in a limited special edition called Reborn PINK. Only 650 of this series of the Crown model were made, in shocking pink. It took no time at all for Toyota's top-of-the-range model in its striking colour to become a cult vehicle.

In addition to the attention-grabbing bodywork, the interior fittings too are out of the ordinary. They were designed by Terry Ito, who is also known as an actor and frequent guest on talk shows. The seats and ceiling are in radiant white. The luxurious dashboard shines in high-class black, set off by fine golden edging and touches of white.

When you take a ride in a Pink Crown, you slide into the soft upholstery and enjoy an almost silent journey in the hybrid-powered car. And when delighted passers-by stop to watch, wave to you and grab their cameras, you will almost feel like a celebrity. So keep an eye open for the pink taxis!

If you don't much like the colour, there is a solution: since 2015 they have been joined by the same model in different colours – gaudy blue or green.

Address Royal-Limousine, Kameido 7-24-1, Koto-ku, 136–0071 Tokyo, call centre +81 (0) 356 276 184 | **Getting there** Tobu-Kameido Line to Kameido-Suijin | **Tip** Two minutes from the train station is Chuo Park, popular with local residents, with something for all generations.

77__The Power Mast
Simply take them down?

Every visitor to Japan notices this phenomenon: the tangled bundles of cables in streets and alleyways, supported every 30 metres or so by a power mast. In fact it is not completely correct to describe them as power masts, as in Japan they are in fact poles, hung about with both power lines and telephone wires.

Over 33 million of them are standing all over the country, and the number is increasing. A government investigation concluded that cities like London and Paris, but also Hong Kong, have put all their cable under the ground, and even in Seoul, 46 per cent of cables are subterranean, but in Tokyo the figure is a paltry 7 per cent – although this process has gone further in the capital city than anywhere else in Japan. Many people regard the overground cables as a plague. It is not just that these suspended tangles spoil the view of sights – a citizens' initiative holds a photo competition to find particularly hideous cases and examples of the opposite, putting them on the Internet. The forest of poles is a hazard in the event of earthquakes and typhoons, as fallen masts can hit passers-by and buildings, and can block the passage of emergency services.

But the battle against the poles is not easy: the costs of underground cabling are 20 times higher, and repairs are much more difficult. Furthermore, many masts not only carry cables but also streetlights, traffic signs, traffic lights and other things that need a post and would be twice as expensive without the use of existing masts.

Thus the removal of masts is going ahead slowly, and primarily in newly constructed complexes. Japan will therefore continue to be a 'great power' as far as cables and masts are concerned, as critics complain.

All the same: don't they sometimes possess a picturesque charm, as in this photo taken in the narrow lanes of Koenji?

Address Koenjikita 3-22-2, Suginami-ku, 166–0002 Tokyo | Getting there JR-Chuo Line (local) and Chuo-Sobu Line to Koenji | Tip The area to the northwest of the station consists of busy lanes with many shops and restaurants. Those of the Okinawan community are very popular.

78__ The Puppet Workshop
Punch and Judy for adults

Very close to trendy Yanaka-Ginza lies Mitsuaki Tsuyuki's puppet workshop. A community of more than 100 hand puppets has already gathered in his studio – and they are no ordinary puppets, but figures with frowning, leering, grinning, expressive faces. Their arms do not dangle loosely by their bodies. On the contrary, their hands seem to be in movement.

The collection is varied. It includes figures with young and old faces, and in addition to those with Japanese features, there are a few that look Western. Some of the characters are immediately recognisable, as the artist has no hesitation about depicting well-known persons from the fields of politics and show business. The former prime minister Junichiro Koizum and the actor and film director Beat Takeshi are among the figures in the gallery of puppets. It is noticeable that the collection mainly consists of older persons, among whom bald-headed men of advanced age are especially numerous. When asked about his preference for such characters, Tsuyuki explains that 'I must be good at doing the facial expression of grandfathers', and gives an embarrassed smile.

The figures in the Shokichi Puppet Workshop are not only there to be looked at. On request Tsuyuki, who was born in 1946, puts them through their paces. If a group of three or more interested visitors is present, the 30-minute show begins. It costs 500 yen per person. Tsuyuki's repertoire extends to sketches with titles such as The Drinker and 50 Years after the Winter Sonata, and calls to mind the age of silent movies.

If you like Tsuyuki's puppets, you can order one from him for a price of 40,000 yen. As a model he requires several photos from different angles of the person who is to be portrayed. You can expect a waiting period of four months: craftsmanship comes at a price and takes time.

Address 指人形笑吉工房, Shokichi Original Hand Puppets, Yanaka 3-2-6, Taito-ku, 110–0001 Tokyo, +81 (0) 338 211 837, shokichi.main.jp (only Japanese) | Getting there Chiyoda metro line to Sendagi, exit to Dango-Zaka, 2-minute walk | **Hours** Wed–Sun 10am–6pm, closed Mon & Tue * | **Tip** The Yanaka-Kohi-Ten coffee shop, where beans are freshly roasted, is easy to find, as the aroma attracts customers before they see it.

79__Retro Town
Back to the future with film posters

About an hour from Shinjuku, in the far west of Tokyo Prefecture, is Ome, a town known to many people at best as a train station where they change on the way to the walking trails in Okutama. To attract visitors, the idea arose of presenting Ome as a 'Showa town', a place with traditional houses and shops in the style of the post-war years. Visitors arriving at the station are greeted by signs in period style. An old-fashioned waiting room is adorned with film posters advertising classic Japanese and international films, and already you feel you have been transported back a few decades. These posters are a recurring element adorning many old buildings all over the town.

But why choose film posters, of all things, when the last of the three cinemas that once operated here closed as long ago as the 1970s? The man behind it all is the artist Noboru Kubo. Born in 1941 in Ome, he has been painting movie posters since he was 19 years old. When the demand for hand-painted cinema advertising declined, he continued with his commercial art, but now for the benefit of his hometown. Now he is in retirement, and students at the local Tama Art School have taken over his work. Posters that have faded with time are replaced with a new one or other works of art. In this way the younger generation, looking back to the traditions of the town, is securing its future.

Take the south exit from the station and turn right to the tourist information office next to the station, where you will get a map showing the locations of all the film posters. As you stroll around this open-air gallery, look out for the remaining old buildings. One of the finest, on the main street, houses a cute little museum that exhibits packaging from the post-war period. And if it rains, you can buy an umbrella from a shop, the front of which is adorned with a billboard advertising *Singin' in the Rain*.

Address 青梅観光案内所, Ome Tourist Information, Honcho 192, Ome-shi, 198−0083 Tokyo | Getting there JR-Ome Line to Ome | Hours Tue–Sun 9.30am–5pm | Tip Drop in at the gallery café Hakoya on the main street opposite the packaging museum. Here you can buy craftwork and get advice, possibly in English, for your tour of Ome.

80__ The Roof of the Kitte
Make it to the top

The district of Marunouchi between the imperial palace, Tokyo train station, Otemachi and Yurakucho has been the financial centre of Japan since the late nineteenth century. At that time, land was sold to private companies, and a modern business district with Western architecture took shape. Despite renewal at various times, the area was in danger of decline in the 1980s, partly because, although there was demand for offices, no more space was available. The solution was to build upwards. Problems of traffic, logistics and the environment also had to be tackled, so the reshaping of Marunouchi was coordinated as a public-private partnership. The older buildings were not simply demolished. Instead the existing fabric was restored and combined with modern skyscrapers.

One of the most interesting of these refurbished buildings is the Kitte. This Japanese word means 'postage stamp', but also 'Come!' It stands diagonally opposite the station. This six-storey structure built in 1933, formerly the main post office for Tokyo, was gutted, its greying façade was cleaned up, and a 38-storey glass tower was placed on top of the whole thing. The new section is largely used to accommodate offices, while today the old part of the building is again home to a post office, as well as an exquisite shopping mall with various specialities from all over Japan, fashion items and restaurants.

The best feature of the Kitte comes last – or rather, right at the top. There is a roof terrace, where office workers can take their lunchtime break or shoppers can recuperate. The panorama allows visitors to admire the redevelopment of Marunouchi: from the thoroughly restored station on the right, across the square in front of the station to the glass giants on the left, standing proud on older buildings, the heart of the country's finance and real-estate sector looks out on a shining future.

Address キッテ, Kitte, JP-Tower, Marunouchi 2-7-2, Chiyoda-ku, 100–0005 Tokyo, www.jptower-kitte.jp | Getting there JR-Chuo Line and others to Tokyo Station | Hours Mon–Fri 11am–11pm, Sat & Sun 11am–10pm, admission free | Tip Around the corner from the Kitte is a replica of the first Mitsubishi office building. Known as the Mitsubishi Ichigokan Museum, it presents changing exhibitions of art and crafts from Japan and Europe.

81_ The Roof Park

A fairground at the top of the town

Tokyo is bursting at the seams. The city is crowded and bustling. Rents for residential and business premises are horrendously high. As there is hardly any space for horizontal expansion in the city centre, shops started to make use of their roofs as long ago as the early twentieth century. Beer gardens, little shrines, gardens and even miniature amusement parks and zoos began to appear on the roofs of stores.

The first roof park was opened by Mitsukoshi in Nihonbashi in 1907. It had a small garden with a pond and a corner with a panoramic view. In 1923 Matsuya in Ginza followed this lead with a zoo. The views from the top of these retail palaces, which are often situated among skyscrapers, is unique and fascinating. What visitors find up on the roof (okujo) is almost always connected with leisure activities. However, as a result of the economic collapse following the 'bubble period' of the late 1980s, many Japanese were forced to reduce their spending, and the leisure facilities on the roofs of shops were less frequented than before. This is why many of the children's rides look a little shabby, and the number of beer gardens has also fallen. Some roof terraces were even closed altogether.

In recent years, retailers have increasingly expanded below ground, as the great advantage of this compared with the roof is that business no longer depends on the whims of the weather and the season. A lot of depachika (literally: under the store) have been built. In addition to restaurants they contain gourmet stands that sell exquisite food.

To save the okujo culture from extinction, a community has formed to campaign for its preservation. Many books and websites show photographs of the golden age of the okujo, so that readers and visitors can indulge in nostalgia. One roof park that is still in good condition is that of the Keio department store in Shinjuku.

Address 京王スカイガーデン, Keio Sky Garden, Nishi-Shinjuku 1-1-4, Shinjuku-ku, 160–8321 Tokyo | Getting there JR-Yamanote Line and others to Shinjuku | Hours Daily 10am–8pm | Tip The more modern roof terrace of Takashimaya department store also provides a good view. Inside, it is worth looking at the DIY shops Tokyu-Hand and Yuzawaya.

82__The Sake Brewery

Rice wine is the best medicine

If you like to enjoy a meal in combination with a fine vintage, you will appreciate having a wide selection of good wines when you dine. Rice wine, too, is an excellent accompaniment to local specialities in Japan. In order to communicate more information about the national drink, some sake breweries organise visits to their production sites and tastings. Ozawa-Shuzo, founded in 1702, is one of these. The company is based in the west of the city in hilly surroundings. The source of the river Tama is close by.

Tours of the brewery are offered daily from 10am. They are free of charge, though the company asks visitors to book in advance. The tours are given in Japanese, but information brochures in English are also available to explain the individual stages of the production process.

There are two restaurants on the site, an unsophisticated one where guests can also sit outside and a higher-class one that serves tofu-based dishes. Sake tastings are held in the fast-food restaurant. The company's brand, Sawanoi, is sold in ten different versions. Depending on the quality, a cup costs between 200 and 500 yen. After the tasting, visitors can take the cup home with them as a souvenir. 'Sawanoi is characterised by a light, dry taste, and therefore goes well with the salty style of Tokyo food,' explained the tour guide, Mr Tsugio Nagasawa. In recent years, however, the company has been making efforts to develop a stronger sake with a unique and unmistakable flavour. Foreign customers, he says, prefer daikarakuchi, an extremely dry rice wine, and a different version with the aroma of apricots is also successful with customers abroad.

Just as doctors in Europe recommend the consumption of wine in moderate quantities, rice wine too is claimed to have health-giving properties. To quote the words of a Japanese proverb: 'Sake is the best of all medicines.'

Address 小澤酒造, Ozawa-Shuzo, Sawai 2-770, Ome-shi, 198-0172 Tokyo, +81 (0) 428 788 215, www.sawanoi-sake.com (only Japanese) | Getting there JR-Ome Line to Sawai, 5-minute walk | Hours Tue–Sun 8am–5pm* | Tip Almost half an hour west along the river, or one stop by train to Ontake, the house of the landscape painter Gyokudo Kawai (1873–1957) lies on a hill in picturesque countryside. The artist's works are shown here in a small museum.

83__ The Screen Museum

From an everyday item to a status symbol

In Japan there are many occasions for setting up a screen. For events such as tea ceremonies, weddings and births, extremely precious screens are made. They are available in a range of sizes: small ones that are no larger than ten centimetres can be purchased and make a popular souvenir, while the larger screens often consist of several folding panels.

The byobu (literally: wind wall) originated in China and was introduced to Japan as long ago as the eighth century. The first ones that were produced still resembled those from China, but in the course of time Japan developed its own techniques, and alterations were made to the structure and design. The materials also changed. Initially, folding screens were covered with silk, which was later replaced by washi (Japan paper). The paper panels are adorned with calligraphy, patterns and paintings.

Over the course of centuries, the screen devised to keep out wind and draughts was increasingly put to other uses and became a symbol expressing the wealth and power of the owner. This trend came to a climax in the samurai period. In that era, the pictorial decoration of screens was particularly colourful, and precious materials such as gold leaf were used.

Today screens are still produced painstakingly by hand in family companies that employ the traditional methods. In Sumida you can visit the only museum in Tokyo that is devoted to this craft. A comprehensive exhibition presents all aspects of the history and production. Examples from all historical periods demonstrate changes in the art over time. Individual stages of production are shown, and tools are on display. Visitors not only gain insights into traditions, but also learn about materials of the future and the uses to which a modern screen can be put in addition to the well-known old applications.

Address 屏風博物館, Museum of Byobu, Mukojima 1-31-6, Sumida-ku, 130–0033 Tokyo, +81 (0) 336 224 470, byoubu-museum.com (only Japanese) | **Getting there** Tobu Sky Tree Line to Tokyo Sky Tree, 5-minute walk | **Hours** Mon–Sat 10am–6pm | **Tip** Visit one of the traditional artisan workshops that are advertised by leaflets in the Museum of Byobu (only in Japanese).

84__ The Sculpture Park

Almost like hunting for Easter eggs

Art in public spaces in Japan did not begin in Tokyo or another large city, but rather in the town of Ube at the southwestern tip of Honshu. There, in a park, the Ube Biennial has taken place since the 1960s.

Other towns followed this lead and installed works of art in open spaces in order to beautify public squares and provide residents with points of identification. In Tokyo too, public art can be found in many places, usually solitary works.

A different approach was taken in the early 1990s in Tachikawa in the west of Tokyo Prefecture. On a large area that was formerly occupied by an American barracks, alongside office and residential complexes, Faret Tachikawa was built – 'fare' is the Italian word for 'to make, create' and 't' stands for Tachikawa. This was accompanied by a liberal provision of art: 109 works by 92 contemporary artists from 36 countries stand, lie or hang here.

Many of the sculptures are not only works of art but also have a practical purpose: Niki de Saint Phalle's contribution, for example, is a bench. Takashi Fukai's chairs are a place to sit, and form a barrier at the same time. Jean-François Brun's sculptures serve as streetlights, and Richard Wilson's stairs are the entrance to a ventilation shaft. The styles, from concrete to abstract art, are as diverse as the applications. Pop art by Claes Oldenburg is represented, as well as minimal art by Donald Judd.

If you would like to have a good look at all of the sculptures, it is best to come in late afternoon when it is still light and to stay until dusk, because then you can also enjoy the light sculptures. An information leaflet (mainly in Japanese) with a map showing the way to all of the works is available from the reception in the library. Then keep your eyes open in every direction, because otherwise it is easy to miss something.

Address ファーレ立川, Faret Tachikawa, Akebono-cho 2-36-2, Tachikawa-shi, 190−0012 Tokyo, www.tachikawa-chiikibunka.or.jp/faretart | Getting there JR-Chuo Line and others to Tachikawa | Hours Library: Mon−Fri 10am−8pm, Sat & Sun 10am−5pm; the sculptures are freely accessible | Tip From the end of the raised pedestrian walkway on the south side of Tachikawa JR station, right by Tachikawa-Minami monorail, you have a fine view of Mount Fuji when the weather is clear.

85__ The Seibu Lions Stadium

Suburban hitters

Baseball was imported to Japan from the USA almost 150 years ago and is one of the country's most popular sports today. Yakyu ('field ball') is not only well loved but is also played to a very high standard. In 2006 the Japanese team succeeded in bringing home the trophy for the World Baseball Classic for the first time, and defended the title three years later. There are two professional divisions, the Central League and the Pacific League. The three best teams from each league compete for the championship at the end of the season.

The Seibu Lions play in the Pacific League. The club was founded in 1978 in Fukuoka, but relocated to Tokorozawa on the edge of Tokyo only one year later. It is owned by the Seibu railway company. To date, the Lions have won the Pacific League 21 times and the Japanese championship 13 times. One of the club's most successful players at present is Shogo Akiyama. He scored 216 hits in the 2015 season alone. This was a world record.

Among the best-known players in the history of the club is the power-hitter Kazuhiro Kiyohara. However, this hero of years past has fallen from a great height: in 2016 Kiyohara was arrested for taking drugs – a huge scandal. One of the best hitters was Takeya Nakamura. He does not have a particularly slim figure, which earned him the nickname 'okawari-kun' (lover of second helpings). Despite his weight, he is agile and moves fast. A previous coach of the team, Hisanobu Watanabe, once said of Nakamura that he held out hope for all fat people. He was a reliable scorer of home runs, but has been out of form since 2016.

Despite having several excellent hitters, the Seibu Lions have not been able to win any titles in recent years. The club changed its coach, and many good players have left the team.

Address 埼玉西武ライオンズ, Saitama Seibu Lions, Kami-Yamaguchi 2135, 359–1153 Tokorozawa, www.seibulions.jp (only Japanese) | Getting there Seibu-Sayama Line from Nishi-Tokorozawa to Seibu-Kyujo-mae | Tip Around the Sayamako and Tamako lakes are broad walking and bike trails in wonderful scenery. The path to them passes the back entrance to the stadium.

86__The Senbei Shop

Fresh and crispy

In a country where rice is the staple food, it is unsurprising that the most popular snack is also made from rice. According to a survey, 83 per cent of Japanese like senbei, a spicy and crispy biscuit made from rice flour.

It has been shown that senbei has been eaten since the eighth century, but it consisted not only of rice, but also of potatoes or wheat. The same is true of sweet baked goods that are also produced under this name, especially in the Kansai region. The hard, salty rice crackers that are so popular originated in a small town called Soka in Saitama Prefecture; this version has existed since the Edo period.

The crispy delicacy can be bought in every supermarket. In the high-class department stores, it is on sale in pretty boxes, because this speciality is also a popular souvenir. Senbei is not made from sticky rice, but from other grains that are then ground and steamed. While it is still hot, the dough is mixed with water, kneaded and poured into moulds. Here it is left until dry. The final stage of the production process is to grill the senbei and then, while it is still warm, to spread on soya sauce or other variations, depending on the flavour that is desired.

Mukashi-Senbei-Daikokuya in Yanaka still makes these rice crackers by hand, and with a little luck you can watch as the last steps of the process are carried out. The business has been operating since 1924, and its equipment looks as if it dates from that time.

The sales counter is right by the pavement. On the right, next to it, in a large, wooden-framed glass case, is a pile of pretty packages containing a variety of different kinds of senbei. On the floor in the middle of the room stands the grill, at which the proprietor turns the rice crackers and spreads sauce on them. The smell of freshly roasted rice biscuits will make your mouth water.

Address 昔せんべい大黒屋, Mukashi-Senbei Daikokuya, Yanaka 1-3-4, Taito-ku, 110–0001 Tokyo, www.nezu-ginza.com/shop/daikokuya | Getting there Chiyoda metro line to Nezu, 4-minute walk | Hours Fri–Wed 10.30am–6.30pm | Tip In addition to many temples in Nippori, 10-minute walk to the west is the Nezu-Jinja Shrine. Its building dates from 1705, and it has an impressive number of bright red tori.

87__ The Sewerage Museum

Under the rainbow

How do things look beneath one of the world's largest cities? How does its sewerage system work? How is flooding prevented when heavy rain falls? Answers to these and many other questions are given at Rainbow sewerage museum in Odaiba.

Even if you might possibly prefer not to know exactly how it looks and smells in a sewer, in a modern city like Tokyo the latest technology is in operation, even below the ground. Insights into a world that otherwise remains hidden from view are both exciting and fascinating.

Visitors to the museum are not only guided through the sewers, but can also attend workshops to learn all about the tasks of the employees who work at the waste-water organisation. At a number of different workstations they can carry out individual tasks themselves. Children can take part in a rally, collecting stamps in a little book: if they succeed in passing through all workstations and thus filling their book with stamps, they are rewarded with a small present.

Visiting the museum is like returning to your schooldays. In the room dedicated to experiments you can find out about the unexpected properties of the element of water. In the water treatment plant at Ariake you learn how drinking water is made from waste water, how the water is conveyed into homes, how it is collected again after use – and much, much more. Further information is communicated by means of films and exhibitions.

Guided tours to give visitors an overall impression are on offer at weekends and on public holidays. It is possible to join a tour without booking in advance. For more comprehensive tours, for example walking through the city's sewers, reservation is essential, however. The institution that calls itself Rainbow may not be an amusement park, but the activities that it offers are equally entertaining – and educational at the same time.

Address 虹の下水道館, Tokyo Sewerage Museum 'Rainbow', Ariake Water
Reclamation Center 5F, Ariake 2-3-5, Koto-ku, 135–0063 Tokyo, +81 (0) 3 556 424 58,
www.nijinogesuidoukan.jp/language/english.html | Getting there Rinkai Line to Odaiba-
Kaihinkoen, 8-minute walk | Hours Tue–Sun 9.30am–4.30pm (last admission 4pm)*;
free admission | Tip At the Tokyo Big Sight trade-fair grounds, the world's biggest comic
fair, Komike, is held twice a year. There are also some architecturally interesting buildings
in this area.

88__Shinbungeiza

A picture house for cineastes

For cinema fans who want to do more than simply consume the latest blockbuster in 3-D quality, and are interested in classic and rarely shown movies, Shinbungeiza is the right place. The programme is devoted equally to films from Japan, Hollywood and the rest of the world.

The cinema was opened by a writer in 1956. In those days there was already a film bookshop and a theatre under the same roof, and from the beginning Shinbungeiza, with its discussion forums, was more than merely a place for screening movies. To this day artists from the film industry, including well-known directors and cinema critics, are invited to events here.

The building had to be demolished in 1997, so after more than 40 years of success, the picture house was forced to close temporarily. A pachinko arcade was opened on the site of the old Shinbungeiza in 2000. The cinema had to move up to the third floor. Despite this closure for a time, the management did not follow the example of modern cinemas but kept faith with the old concept. The admission prices are extremely low by Tokyo standards, and a ticket is valid in general for two screenings. If you only attend the last screening, the price is lower.

The night specials are extremely popular. They are on offer on Wednesdays and Saturdays, and are called all-night shows. Usually they have a theme. It might be a series of animes one day, and films that are linked by a common theme the next time. Some night showings are dedicated to the work of a particular actor or director.

Shinbungeiza has retained the old-fashioned charm that once constituted the appeal of spending an evening at the cinema. The screenings are accompanied by flickering and humming noises.

Perfect technical quality would be out of place here. This is precisely why numerous fans who have grown old along with this cinema still love to come here.

Address 新文芸座, Shinbungeiza, Higashi-Ikebukuro 1-43-5, Toshima-ku, 170–0013 Tokyo, www.shin-bungeiza.com (only Japanese) | **Getting there** JR-Yamanote Line and others to Ikebukuro, east exit, 3-minute walk | **Tip** The Seibu and Tobu department stores by the station were Japan's longest buildings for many years and they are still magnets for visitors – in 2015, after its refurbishment, Seibu achieved a record number of 70 million visitors.

89__ The Shinmei Shrine

The dolls' cemetery

There is a tradition for Girls' Day in March of setting up dolls' shrines in houses. The hina dolls that appear on this occasion are very valuable. They are brought out one or two weeks before the event, and then put away again afterwards. According to a popular saying, a girl who is not able to part from her dolls will later never find a husband.

Sooner or later they lose interest in their hina dolls anyway. Then the time has come to part once and for all from these precious playthings. In some cases they are passed on to grandchildren, but usually the bulky cases in which they are kept clutter a family's cramped rented accommodation, and the dolls are thrown away long before the girls have reached adulthood.

As the dolls are important companions in the early phases of a child's life, and were received as presents from grandparents in most cases, they are of great personal value, and most people are not willing simply to dispose of them with the normal household waste. For this reason there are shrines that offer 'ningyo-kuyo', the ritual burning of the hina dolls. On payment of a fee the entire set of hina figures, as well as all other kinds of dolls and cuddly toys, can be handed in there all year round.

At Shinmeisha in Tokorozawa, dolls that have outlived their usefulness are stored, clearly visible to visitors, in a little house with a glass façade. Once a year, on the first Sunday in June, the dolls are burned. The ceremony begins at 9am. For the purpose of a last farewell, the girls' faithful friends are displayed on sheets and benches. The thought that these treasures will no longer delight the hearts of children can make you feel wistful. When the ceremony of dancing, singing and prayer has concluded, the priest lights the bonfire. The event ends for spectators when the first batch of dolls has been burned.

Address 所沢神明社, Tokorozawa-Shinmei-Shrine, Miyamoto-cho 1-2-4, 359–1143 Tokorozawa | Getting there Seibu-Shinjuku Line to Kokukoen (local), 6-minute walk | Tip Behind the Shinmei Shrine lies the old quarter of Tokorozawa.

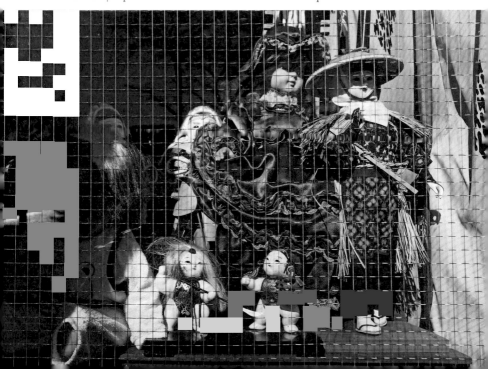

90___Showa-Kinen Park

More than cherry blossom and ginkgo avenues

Everyone who has lived in Tokyo for a while will surely have paid a visit to Showa-Kinen Park. Most people go there in springtime to see the cherry blossom or in autumn to admire the golden avenues of ginkgos. An estimated 80 per cent of visitors enter the extensive park through the main gate. By the time they reach the big grassy playground in the middle of the park, most begin to feel tired, and then the unwelcome thought that they have to walk all the way back slowly creeps into their minds. Have you experienced the park in this way? If so, you have not yet got to know the best spots in Tokyo's biggest green space, a site that used to be a base for the American armed forces.

The next time you go, take one of the side entrances or, even better, hire a bike. Then you are mobile and can explore every corner of the park without effort. Close to the Sunagawa exit there is a small open-air museum, where an old farm from the Musashino Plain has been reconstructed. Here visitors learn how people practised agriculture in harmony with nature. A few hundred metres further on is the Japanese garden with its bonsai section. There is a wonderful panoramic view of the lake. In the teahouse, tea ceremonies are held several times daily on the second Sunday in the month.

For families with children a wide range of facilities has been provided. The largest playground is at the 'Kodomo-no-Mori'. To get an overview of the playground, the best idea is to climb to the top of the sun pyramid. There are bouncy castles, the biggest hammock in the whole of Japan for the kids to climb around in, a long slide and much more to delight a child's heart – in the dragon park, for example, children clamber about on these primeval monsters. Showa-Kinen Park is a place that you can visit often and at any time of the year without fear of being bored.

Address 国営昭和記念公園, Showa-Kinen-Park, Midori-cho 3173, Tachikawa-shi, 190−0015 Tokyo, www.showakinen-koen.jp | Getting there JR-Ome Line to Nishi-Tachikawa, 2-minute walk | Hours Mar−Oct 9.30am−5pm, Nov−Feb 9.30am−4.30pm | Tip At the main entrance is a structure that has been built into the hill−well worth a look.

91__The Souvenir Shop

Reminders of verbal acrobats and cats

The Yanaka district is highly popular with foreign tourists because many survivals from traditional Japan can still be discovered there. To find out more about the history of this area, it is worth visiting Tamaru. This shop is a veritable treasure trove, as it stocks many omiyage (souvenirs) that are associated with the district.

Rakugo is a storyteller's art that originated in Yanaka and is based on comic monologues. The narrator amuses his audience by means of exaggerated emphasis and humorous gestures. Mr Ogawa, the owner of Tamaru, relates the circumstances that caused him to establish his business: 'My daughter and I were looking around for a business idea when by chance we met Mrs Minobe, the daughter of a well-known master of rakugo. She told us that she would like to have a place where she would be reminded of her deceased father.' The result of this encounter was that his shop Tamaru is the only one in the whole of Tokyo that sells rakugo articles.

Yanaka is famous not only for its verbal acrobats, but also for its cats. The living ones are joined by feline figures that greet visitors from the roofs or window shutters. In many souvenir shops, cats are reproduced on textile products, bags, T-shirts and ornaments made from every imaginable material. Thanks to this peculiarity, Yanaka has become known all over Japan as 'neko no machi' (cat town). In Tamaru as in the other shops you will find a wide range of souvenirs in feline form. In addition to the familiar white cat that brings good luck, there are figures of the 'original Yanaka cat', which also raises its paw, but has a more rounded shape than its famous sister animal.

The most valuable item that you can buy at Tamaru is a netsuke, a small weight carved from wood. In the days when the kimono was still an everyday garment, a netsuke was used to close a money bag.

Address 多満留, Tamaru, Yanaka 3-11-15, Taito-ku, 110−0001 Tokyo, +81 (0) 358 144 425 |
Getting there JR-Yamanote Line and others to Nippori, west exit, 5-minute walk | **Hours**
Tue−Sun 11am−7pm* | **Tip** Next to Tamaru a small café with the same name is run by the
wife of the shop owner. Here you can try local specialities such as goma-dango (skewered
dumplings with black sesame sauce).

92___The Star Hiroba

Aluminium plaques instead of marble stars

In Hollywood it is called the Walk of Fame, and in Tokyo the name is Star-Hiroba, the artists' square in Asakusa.

Many celebrated persons from past times came from this area. The arts of kabuki, rakugo, comedy and enka (Japanese pop music) were well represented here. To commemorate this tradition, the square dedicated to performing artists was inaugurated in 1979. Two criteria for inclusion apply: the artists honoured here must have worked in the entertainment business and have been born in the Taito district.

In front of the entrance to the Asakusa Kokaido Theatre is a gallery of artists, let into the pavement. Aluminium plaques measuring 30 centimetres are lined up. On them the hand prints and autographs of selected stars can be seen. Every year five more are added, chosen by a jury. The collection has now grown to include almost 300 squares of aluminium.

Of all the artists whose names are recorded here, the film director and actor Takeshi Kitano (Beat Takeshi) is probably the one best known to people outside Japan. Nevertheless it is worth taking a look at the careers of the other famous people, for example that of the kabuki actor Kanzaburo Nakamura, who has had a decisive influence on this genre of theatre in the twenty-first century. With his group, named Heisei-Nakamura-za, he gained an international reputation and has often appeared on television and in films. The folk singer Hibari Misora had a status like that of Edith Piaf in her homeland when she was active. Sachiko Kobayashi, today a highly successful enka singer and presenter, came from a poor background and had to struggle for many years to gain recognition in her field. A further hand print that can be found in the celebrity gallery of 'Taitowood' belongs to Yoji Yamada, the director of a popular series called *Torasan* (It's Tough Being a Man).

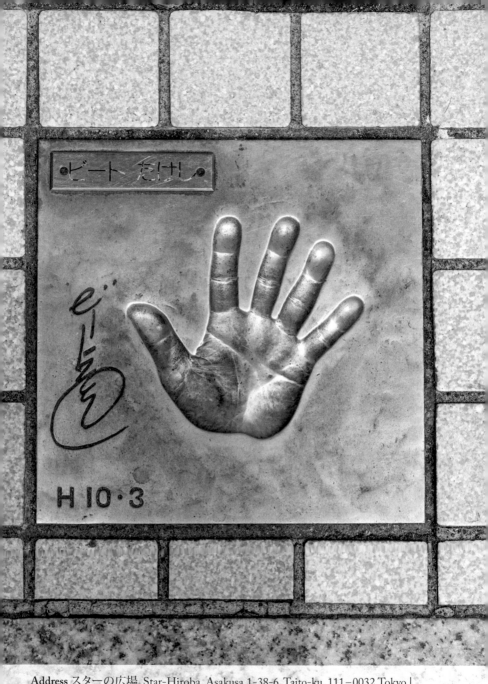

Address スターの広場, Star-Hiroba, Asakusa 1-38-6, Taito-ku, 111–0032 Tokyo |
Getting there Ginza metro line to Asakusa, exits 1 and 3, 5-minute walk | **Tip** Very close to
the Star-Hiroba in Denpoin-dori is a kimono shop called Konjaku-Kimono, which
has a large selection of low-cost second-hand garments.

93__ The Swimming Pool

Pack your swimwear

In summer, when the thermometer rises above 30 degrees Celsius, a lot of people in Tokyo have only one thing in mind: they long to cool down and feel refreshed. A large proportion of the inhabitants of this city of nine million then set off for one of the few open-air pools, with results that are sometimes bizarre. If you would like to avoid the masses, it is recommended not to go swimming in the O-Bon period in August, when most Japanese take a holiday from work. At other times, too, when the weather is hot during the school holidays and at weekends, the pools can be overcrowded. On the other hand, if the sky is cloudy and the temperatures not quite so high, the all-weather pools are often scenes of emptiness, even during the high season.

The Seibuen Yuenchi Pool lies at the edge of the city, between Tokyo and Saitama Prefecture. Thanks to several attractions for visitors, cooling-off in the water here is the ultimate in bathing: the pool has a wave machine, no fewer than six tube-like water chutes and the so-called nagare pool, in which swimmers drift gently through the water, drawn by the pull of the current. Several paddling pools are available for small children.

One of the regulations may seem strange to foreigners: to ensure that everything runs smoothly during the peak season, for safety reasons all swimmers have to leave the water for 5 minutes, once every 30 minutes. When the pool superintendent blows a whistle, you should leave the pool without delay.

Since 2016 there have been moonlight swimming sessions in this pool. The colourful lights of the adjacent amusement park, reflected on the surface of the water, create a magical mood. This event is called the night pool. In its first year it happened only on Fridays, and every day during the O-Bon period. Depending on the number of visitors, there may be changes to the opening hours.

Address 西武園遊園地プール, Seibuen Yuenchi Pool, Yamaguchi 2964, 359–1145 Tokorozawa, +81 (0) 429 221 371, www.seibuen-yuuenchi.jp/information (only Japanese) | **Getting there** Seibuen Line to Seibuen, 5-minute walk | **Hours** Daily 9am–5pm, night pool Fri and O-Bon period daily 5–9pm (swimming season is early July to early Sept) | **Tip** Seibu-Yuenchi amusement park is on the same site. For admission to both, you can save money by buying a combined ticket.

94___Takahata-Fudo
Buddhist, though not Zen

Buddhism is not the same as Zen, although in the West the two are often equated. There is a tradition of various streams in Buddhism that are much older. Zen did not appear until the twelfth century, and before that time the Shingon School, which arrived from India via China in the eighth century, and the Tendai School characterised the Buddhism of the Heian period. Both of these schools have large, magnificent temples, whereas the sacred precincts of Zen Buddhism are often small and plain.

Takahata-Fudo, which is officially called Kongo-ji, belongs to the Shingon sect, as do two other temples described in this book, Fukagawa-Fudo-do and Yamaguchi-Canon. The temple grounds cover a huge area. Part of it is the mountain Takahata, through which Kongo-ji received its popular name. About 1,100 years ago a temple was constructed on the mountain, which is in fact more like a hill. As the first structure was swept away by a typhoon in the twelfth century, it was rebuilt in a more secure place lower down. The characteristic landmark of the temple grounds is a tall pagoda, newly built in the style of the Heian period.

The main hall, the Fudo-do, houses a sculpture weighing 1,100 kilogrammes and depicting Fudo-Myo, the protector of the temple, and his followers. For the 1,000-year jubilee, replicas of the figures, faithful to the originals, were made, but here too several exhibits date from the Heian period. The ceiling painting of a gigantic dragon has existed since the Edo period. The guardians at the entrance, called Nio, have also survived the passage of several centuries without damage. Visitors can discover the whole temple grounds by following a specially designated route. At 88 stations the famous pilgrims' path of Kukai, the founder of Shingon, can be traced without having to cover the 1,200-kilometre-long original route on the island of Shikoku.

Address 高幡不動, Takahata-Fudo, Takahata 733, Hino-shi, 191 – 0031 Tokyo, www.takahatafudoson.or.jp | **Getting there** Tama monorail or Keio Line to Takahata-Fudo | **Hours** Daily 9am – 5pm | **Tip** In the temple grounds a flea market for antiques, crafts and other old things is held every third Sunday in the month from 7am – 4pm.

95 __ The Tamagawa Aqueduct
Water for a thirsty city

The place that is now Tokyo was once an idyllic fishing village called Edo. In 1603 the shogun, Ieyasu Tokugawa, decided to found a new capital city here. The settlement grew with enormous speed. At the beginning of the eighteenth century, Edo had a population of more than one million. Since this time the city, renamed Tokyo in 1868, has been one of the largest in the world.

As the inhabitants needed supplies of water for drinking and extinguishing fires, the shogun ordered the construction of a dam in the river Tama on the Musashino Plateau, at a distance of 40 kilometres from the capital. The brothers Shoemon and Seiemon, under the supervision of the ruler of the city of Kawagoe, Nobutsuna Matsudaira, were given the task of building the dam and a canal. Construction work started in 1653, and the aqueduct was completed in only 18 months. The brothers, who were ordinary farmers before they received this huge commission, were honoured for their outstanding work, and henceforth were permitted to bear the surname Tamagawa. A monument to the two stands in Hamura Park.

Before this system of water supply was completed, the only source was the Kanda Aqueduct, which was inadequate to meet demand. A canal with a length of 43 kilometres was built. It starts in present-day Hamura and ends in the city centre at the Okido Gate in Yotsuya. In some places the aqueduct is extremely narrow, but it always carries enough water for the flow to reach its destination.

The Tamagawa Canal is a good place to get away from the bustle of the big city for a while. The section close to Tamagawajosui train station is especially beautiful. Luxuriant vegetation and the splashing of the water have a calming effect. You can take a wonderful walk or ride a bike along the canal bank. Since 2003, the aqueduct has been recognised as a national historical landmark.

Address 玉川上水, Tamagawajosui, Saiwai-cho 6-36-1, Tachikawa-shi, 190−0002 Tokyo | Getting there Seibu-Haijima Line and others to Tamagawajosui | Tip In the Kawagoedo-Ryokuchi woodland stands a kominka, an old residence of middle-class citizens that can be visited free of charge.

96__ The Todoroki Valley
Power spot and wish fulfilment

For a green oasis where you can escape the noise and stress of the big city, take a trip to the Todoroki valley in Setagaya. It is the only valley in the middle of Tokyo and can be reached after just a few minutes' walk from Todoroki train station. Close to the golf bridge, steep steps lead down to a fascinating jungle-like world overgrown with vegetation.

The gorge is one kilometre long and up to 109 metres deep. Apart from the calls of birds and the cicadas in summer, and the babbling of the brook, it is very quiet here. The sounds of the city of millions seem to be hundreds of miles away. A narrow path leads along the river Yanazawa.

The Todoroki valley has been named a 'power spot' by Japanese travel guidebooks. Many people in Japan, especially women, suffer from stress at their place of work or have difficulties in combining their family life with their job. They are possibly unhappy in their relationship or have not found a partner at all. There is now a trend for people who are searching for happiness to make a pilgrimage to places that have been defined as power spots. A walk in the Todoroki valley is said to bring about a physical and psychological cleansing. Meditation at the waterfall at the end of the valley is said to be particularly recommended. Touching its shallow jet is said to assist in finding new spiritual energy.

Close to the waterfall, steps lead upwards. If you follow this path, you come to the Todoroki-Fudo, a temple dating from the Heian period. A visit to this sacred place is also highly recommended, as it is said to put new life into a loving relationship and at the same time improve performance at school. Whether the site can fulfil all of the high expectations placed in it is something that visitors have to decide for themselves. But anyone who simply wants to be exposed to positive energy will surely not be disappointed.

Address 等々力渓谷, Todoroki valley, Todoroki 1-22, Setagaya-ku, 158–0082 Tokyo |
Getting there Tokyu-Oimachi Line (local) to Todoroki, 3-minute walk | Tip Follow
the river Yanazawa at the end of the valley to reach the river Tamagawa after about ten
minutes, where you have a sweeping view. More walks begin from here.

97 — Tonogayato-Teien
Diverse landscapes in a small space

In Japan there are two kinds of garden, to put it in simple terms: small ones that are admired from a building and large landscape gardens that are meant for walking through. Of the second kind, several examples dating from the Edo period remain, for example Koishikawa-Korakuen. It is one of a group of establishments owned by daimyo, provincial princes, in the capital. In contrast to symmetrical baroque gardens, they consist of several parts: expanses of lawn, woodland, a lake and 'mountains', which can only be viewed from the carefully planned paths and provide a series of surprising, unexpected perspectives.

After the Edo period the people who could afford landscape gardens such as Tonogayato were rich businessmen. In this case the family that founded Mitsubishi bought the estate in 1929. They completed the garden, which had been started in 1913, and added buildings in which the family lived until 1974. After this, protests by local residents persuaded Tokyo Prefecture to not use the garden as land for building but to take it over and open it to the public in 1979.

A circuit of Tonogayato begins on a meadow with a row of sycamore trees whose leaves turn a wonderful, glowing red in autumn. If you follow the path straight ahead, you come to a passage made from bamboo poles, up which purple wisteria grows in spring. The path now descends into a valley, passing a bamboo grove on the right and a small, hilly wood on the left. Beyond a bend, which deliberately blocks the view, you reach the most beautiful spot in the garden: a view of a small waterfall from the banks of a carp pond. Above this, a steep slope leads up to a teahouse, from where you have a panoramic view across the pond and the woods behind it. All that is lacking to make the atmosphere perfect is for a few elderly ladies wearing kimonos to play music with their koto (zithers).

Address 殿ヶ谷戸庭園, Tonogayato Gardens, Minami-machi 2-16, Kokubunji-shi, 185–0021 Tokyo, teien.tokyo-park.or.jp/en/tonogayato | **Getting there** JR-Chuo Line and others to Kokubunji, 2-minute walk | **Hours** Daily 9am–5pm | **Tip** On the way to the station you will find a huge choice of burgers that you won't get at the big chains at This Is The Burger.

98__ The Totoro Woods

Home of the cuddly monster

The anime *My Neighbour Totoro* by Hayao Miyazaki was an international success in 1988. Almost every child In Japan is the proud owner of the wood monster in the shape of a cuddly toy, or the cat bus, or one of the cute balls of dust from the film. No wonder people want to know where these strange creatures are at home. Miyazaki himself revealed that he took inspiration for his story from a grove of trees in Sayama and the countryside around it. Before that, this area, which was disparagingly described by ill-wishers as a sleepy dump, only called to mind the green tea for which the district is known.

In Sayama time truly seems to have stood still. Almost 30 years after Miyazaki paid a visit to the region, almost nothing appears to have changed. When taking a walk through the hilly landscape, passing woods, lakes, small temples and tea plantations, you feel you are being transported back to the time of the film. And if the wind then rustles the leaves, you might think you are hearing the bright voices of Saki and Mei. With a little bit of luck, some of those who take a stroll here might happen on a sign bearing the faces of the one large totoro and the two small ones while exploring the area. This plaque is a reference to the woodland that was given the name Totoro-no-Mori (Totoro's Forest) in honour of the filmmaker Hayao Miyazaki.

Apart from this, no signposts are to be seen, and it is therefore no easy matter to track down the haunts of the woodland monster. It would surely not reflect Miyazaki's intentions if the place that once inspired him were to degenerate into a tourist attraction. Nevertheless, if you have a little patience and are open to the atmosphere here, you might just chance upon the right track – and if you don't, well that doesn't matter because, as they say in Japan, what matters is making the journey, not arriving.

Address トトロの森, Totoro's Forest, Kami-Yamaguchi Zakoiri 351, 359–1153 Tokorozawa, www.totoro.or.jp/totorofund/index.html | **Getting there** Seibu-Sayama Line from Nishi-Tokorozawa to Seibu-Kyujo-mae, 20-minute walk | **Tip** If you follow the road up the hill for about ten minutes you will reach the Italian restaurant Adriano, which is popular, especially among Japanese women, for its welcoming atmosphere and delicious cakes.

99 _ The Traditional Teahouse
Cosy Japan

It is the hidden oases that constitute the charm of the city of Tokyo. Many of these places are found by chance or through some helpful person who would like to do you a favour. Kosoan is a special place of this kind, just waiting to be discovered. It is an old, traditional house, tucked out of the way in a side street in Jiyugaoka. There is no sign in English to indicate that one of Tokyo's loveliest teahouses is concealed inside.

When you have closed the glass sliding door behind you, slipped off your shoes and taken a seat on the tatami at one of the low tables, you will immediately feel that you have entered a different world.

There is plenty to look at here: the room is decorated with old paintings, swords, ceramics and dolls. The picture window looks out onto a wonderful Zen garden.

Now you can enjoy the quiet atmosphere over a cup of matcha, the famous green powdered tea, perhaps accompanied by a wagashi, a traditional sweet cake that is made from rice flour and bean paste. As an alternative to matcha tea, which is rather bitter, you may like to try a fresh strawberry or banana milk shake. An English-language menu with photos of the dishes makes it easier to decide what to order. Highly recommended is anmitsu, a soup made from red beans and syrup, then served with fresh fruit and warabi-mochi (small white dumplings, made using the starch from ferns). The speciality of the house is matcha-zenzai, small rice dumplings floating in tea. Beneath the green soup there lies a layer of anko, the red bean paste. The bitter tea and the sweet paste join in perfect harmony, in terms of both their colour and their taste.

Kosoan is more than just a teahouse. It is also a venue for cultural events. Exhibitions are held here regularly, and performances of traditional arts. Antique hina dolls are on display on Girls' Day.

Address 古桑庵, Kosoan, Jiyugaoka 1-24-23, Meguro-ku, 152–0035 Tokyo, +81 (0) 337 184 203, www.kosoan.co.jp (only Japanese) | Getting there Tokyu-Toyoko Line and others to Jiyugaoka, main exit, 5-minute walk | Hours Thu–Tue 11am–6.30pm | Tip Close by, on a small square named La Vita in reference to Venice, are several restaurants and shops, including one that sells unusual clothing for dogs.

100_ The Train Library
Sidelined, but not useless

In the middle of a high-rise housing estate in Higashi-Murayama stands an old yellow train carriage that has been retired from service. It houses a library for children. The history of Tokyo's only train library goes back to 1967. In those days there was not yet a public library in this district, so the local community was presented with the old railway carriage by the Seibu train company to serve the purpose. When the Green Town estate was built on the same site in 1987, the library had to be moved. Since 1974 there had been a public library building in Higashi-Murayama, so the old carriage had done its duty and was no longer needed.

It often happens that something is not truly appreciated until, all of a sudden, it is no longer there. This was the case in Higashi-Murayama. The local residents soon missed their book train. For them it was not merely a facility where they borrowed something to read, but also an indispensable place for meeting other people. The local district council therefore made efforts to get hold of a new train carriage.

In 2001 they were finally successful. The new out-of-service carriage accommodates more than 5,000 children's books. It is much more than a library: it is also a place for meeting friends and playing. Adults organise readings and craftwork courses for the children here. The most important thing, however, is the atmosphere of bygone days. The children get to know a piece of the past that had almost been forgotten.

People outside Higashi-Murayama heard about this neighbourhood project through the film *Sweet Bean*. Their curiosity was aroused, and they came to see it. The initiators warmly welcome anyone who is genuinely interested in the book train, but also request that visitors respect the privacy of the young users and the volunteers who run the project.

Address くめがわ電車図書館, Kumegawa-Densha-Toshokan, Misumi-cho 1-4-1, Higashi-Murayama-shi, 189–0023 Tokyo | **Getting there** Seibu-Tamako Line to Yasaka, 10-minute walk | **Hours** Wed 10am–noon & 2–4.30pm, Sat 2–4.30pm | **Tip** The River Karabori flows through Higashi-Murayama. For Boys' Day, koinobori (carp banners made from fabric) are hung over the river from the end of April at the Green Town estate.

101_ The Ultraman Arcade

The birthplace of Superman's Japanese brother

In Japan there are more than 12,000 shopping arcades, known as shotengai. Typically they are alleys with shops on both sides, sometimes under cover, without car traffic. At the ends of these streets there often stand arches or gates bearing the name of the shopping mall. As a result of increasing competition from complexes in train stations and gigantic shopping centres, today you often see rows of stores that are mainly closed up and shuttered. The associations of these arcades, formed to represent the shop owners, therefore come up with all sorts of ideas to keep their customers and attract new ones. One good example of this trend arose in 2005 through a merger of three such associations to form the Ultraman shotengai around the station at Odakyu-Soshigaya.

But who is Ultraman, and what has he got to do with Soshigaya? Ultraman is a superhero, half alien, half Japanese. He first appeared on Japanese television in 1966 to save the world from galactic threats – a mission that he and his comrades still pursue in films, video games and live-action shows. The creator of Ultraman, the company Tsuburaya Productions, was originally based in this district.

Now you can admire sculptures from the realm of this icon of Japanese pop culture in his 'home'. One figure stands guard in front of the station, in a characteristic pose with his arms akimbo, while another, 'flying' on an arch, marks the entrance to the shopping arcade. The streetlights also appear in Ultraman look, and on the Internet you can find information about events relating to Ultraman.

If you have now been gripped by Ultraman fever, you can buy every imaginable item of merchandising in several shops in the shotengai, eat your fill of Ultraman sweets or, to drown your sorrows at the fact that you don't have superhuman powers yourself, drink some Ultraman sake.

Address ウルトラマン商店街, Ultraman Shopping Mall, Soshigaya 1-8-11, Setagaya-ku, 157–0072 Tokyo, www.ultraman-shotengai.com | **Getting there** Odakyu-Odawara Line (local) to Soshigaya-Okura | **Hours** Shops: daily 9am–8pm; sculptures: always accessible | **Tip** About 20-minute walk from the station, in the large Setagaya Park, the Setagaya exhibition hall displays its own collection and interesting shows by international and Japanese artists.

102 __ The Underground Tour

Paradise for vampires

Would you like to get properly lost? If so, the subterranean connections in and around Tokyo train station are just the ticket. In these pedestrian tunnels you can explore a large area between Otemachi, Yurakucho and Hibiya, between Ginza and Nihonbashi, without ever having to emerge into daylight.

The network of passages began to grow in the pre-war years, originally as a way of connecting different stations and making it easier to change trains. Links to large office buildings and shops were added, thus creating a chaotic, heterogeneous labyrinth: in some places you glide through elegant, modern cellars on escalators, in others you have to weave your way along cramped, worn-down passages.

You can also go shopping below ground: subterranean rovers can buy everything here, from clothes to food. One particularly interesting store is Character Dori beneath the Yaesu side of Tokyo station. Here a major broadcaster sells merchandise items for fans of popular characters from its anime series. A further unexpected discovery is the magnificent hall beneath Yurakucho station. The opportunities for eating and drinking are also varied: you can consume noodles standing up or take a seat in a high-class restaurant.

If you would like your tour to cover a considerable distance, try the three-kilometre-long route from Otemachi to Higashi-Ginza. You definitely need patience, as it is easy to lose your bearings underground, and it is only possible to give an approximate description of the route here: from Otemachi follow the signs towards JR-Tokyo station. Next you continue through the Tokyo Forum to Yurakucho. Here you reach the Yurakucho Itocia store and enter a passage at right angles that takes you right to Hibiya station and then left to Higashi-Ginza. If all of this works out, you will emerge into daylight right next to the kabuki theatre.

Address 東京駅, Tokyo Station, Marunouchi 1-9-1, Chiyoda-ku, 100–0005 Tokyo | Getting there Various lines to Tokyo station | Tip The Tokyo Station Gallery puts on good changing exhibitions and provides interesting views of the beautifully restored station.

103__ The UR Agency

Housing yesterday, today and tomorrow

The Museum of the History of Housing Estates (Shugojutaku-Rekishi-Kan) in Hachioji informs its visitors about changes in the field of public housing over a period of more than 80 years. For a long time, this was the only section of this information centre that was open to the general public. In recent years, however, it has also been possible for everyone to view exhibitions on subjects such as ecology and safety in the construction industry.

The Urban Renaissance Agency, UR Agency for short, has a leading role in urban development. Its task is to improve living conditions in housing estates (danchi). Sustainability is an important aspect of this. In this connection such issues as how to use resources more economically and reducing waste are tackled. Smaller measures like the collection and use of rainwater or creating more green spaces, for example on roofs, are taken into consideration. The agency also investigates new building materials that may last longer than conventional ones, and research is carried out into new technologies that do not pose a hazard to the environment. Demonstrations of many themes connected with ecology can be seen in the 'sustainability building'.

The safety of residential buildings is also part of the duties of the institute. Japan is frequently affected by natural disasters such as earthquakes and typhoons. Wind is also a factor to be taken into account, as modern housing is being built taller and taller. To minimise the risk of severe damage through environmental factors, the UR Agency has developed unique methods of research and means of construction, which are presented to visitors who visit the museum.

The aim is to make modern residential accommodation more attractive, safer and more comfortable, but not to the detriment of the environment – a challenge that constitutes the task of the UR Agency.

Address 都市再生機構 都市住宅技術研究, Urban Renaissance Agency, Ishikawacho 2683-3, Hachioji-shi, 192−0032 Tokyo, +81 (0) 426 443 751, annai01@ur-net.go.jp, www.ur-net.go.jp/rd/english | **Getting there** JR-Hachiko Line to Kita-Hachioji, 10-minute walk | **Hours** Mon−Fri 1.30−5.30pm, last admission 4.30pm; by appointment only; visitors who do not speak Japanese should take someone along who can interpret for them | **Tip** Tofuya-Ukai-Owada, an exquisite tofu restaurant, lies only ten minutes' walk from the institute in a wonderful Japanese garden.

104__The Village Experience
Art, culture and nature

Have you always wanted to find out the secrets of origami? Or do you enjoy making merry little gnomes out of acorns and pine cones? This village is exactly the right place for all lovers of craftwork.

At weekends craft workshops are held at Hachikokuyama-Taiken-no-Sato. The themes are usually related to the season of the year. Telephone in advance to find out about programmes and dates. Origami paper and materials from the woods are provided free of charge. For the use of leather and metal, a small fee has to be paid. While a member of staff explains how to proceed with more complicated tasks, for simpler activities such as scissor-cutting silhouettes there are sets of instructions, in which everything is shown in diagrams, step by step. The staff are friendly and pleased to help if anyone gets stuck with their work. Other participants in the course, often from an older age group, assist if someone has difficulty in following the instructions, and help until you have really mastered all the steps in the work.

At the back of the building is an exhibition dedicated to the lives of people in the past in the Sayama region. Among the highlights are several exhibits from the Jomon era, which are rarely to be seen in Japan. On the grounds of the village, close to the entrance, there stands a small white building with a gabled roof. This is a traditional storehouse, known as a kura, of which several have survived in this area.

If you would like to stretch your legs for a little while after taking part in the cultural activities, the woods of Hachikokuyama are a suitable place for taking a lengthy walk. This swathe of forest serves as the border between two prefectures, those of Tokyo and Saitama. The hilly countryside as you approach the woodland is very picturesque, and it is especially beautiful in this area when the cherry trees are in blossom in spring.

Address 八国山たいけんの里, Hachikokuyama-Taiken-no-Sato, Noguchicho 3-48-1, Higashi-Murayama-shi, 189–0022 Tokyo, +81 (0) 423 902 161 | **Getting there** Seibuen Line to Seibuen, 8-minute walk | **Hours** Wed–Sun 9.30am–5pm (last admission 4.30pm)*, admission free | **Tip** The nearby Kitayama Park is a source of varied motifs for photographers all year round, especially when the iris are in flower in June.

105__ The Wax Model Shop
Looks good, tastes good

Replicas of meals are a Japanese invention. Their purpose is to make the beholder's mouth water. This appetising fake food is an encouragement to enter a restaurant. For tourists especially, who do not speak the language or are not familiar with the diversity of Japanese cooking, these models, made true to the original dish, are helpful in making a decision.

Nowadays the models are not only found in the windows and showcases of restaurants, but have also become popular gifts to bring home to friends and family.

You will find an inexhaustible array of dummy food at Ganso Sample Ya. The shop stocks models that can be exhibited somewhere as decoration as well as useful items such as key rings, dispensers for rolls of sticky tape, little boxes and much more.

Takizo Iwasaki (1895–1965), the founder of Ganso Sample Ya, made his first food model in 1932. It was an omelette. In those days he still used wax. Since the mid-1920s the demand for wax models had grown rapidly, because more and more restaurant owners used them to advertise their wares. Between the 1970s and 1980s, Iwasaki's company gradually replaced wax, which was not heat-resistant and whose colour faded easily, with a rubber-like material, the shelf-life of which is much, much longer. Silicon is highly suitable for modelling intricate details.

Ganso Sample Ya does not restrict its activities to making replicas of meals. For customers who like to work with their hands, it puts on workshops to teach them how to make the models for themselves, with expert guidance. As these courses have proved to be a massive hit with the foreign community, all of the information is available in English.

Model kits are available for those who prefer to do the work at home, and a huge range of products can also be ordered online.

Address 元祖サンプル屋, Ganso Food Sample Shop, Nishi-Asakusa 3-7-6, Taito-ku, 111–0035 Tokyo, +81 (0) 120 171 839, www.ganso-sample.com/en | **Getting there** Tsukuba-Express Line to Asakusa, exit A 2; 5-minute walk | **Hours** Daily 10am–5.30pm | **Tip** Ganso Sample Ya is in Kappabashi-Dori, a district where you will find many shops selling items for restaurants. It is worth strolling and taking a look around.

106__The Wholesale Market
Market traders and bargains

For a place where you can watch traders bargaining and do some shopping for yourself at low prices, go to the Higashi-Kurume wholesale market. There you will find almost every kind of food used in Japanese cooking. The customers are both retailers and restaurant owners – some of whom are very critical.

One regular is Mr Morishita, a chef who is responsible for the meals at a private school. For many years he has come to the market every morning at six o'clock to select only the very best ingredients for the day's menu. 'Nowhere else are the fish and meat as fresh as here', he reveals.

Take a leisurely stroll down the long aisles of the market hall and watch the lively goings-on. In Higashi-Kurume you are not confined to watching: you can also buy at the stalls. Private customers are expressly welcome, and those who book in advance by telephone can have a guided tour in Japanese.

The items on sale are not only foodstuffs. You can also purchase all kinds of household goods and cleaning equipment, boxes to keep foodstuffs fresh or paper plates for your next party. At the shop called Tanaka-Shoji you will find all kinds of products for packaging and decoration. There are wonderfully kitschy plastic garlands with sakura or grape motifs. Cute little teddy bears and figures like Kumamon, the bear mascot of Kumamoto Prefecture, are perfect for decorating tables at a children's birthday party. Shimada-Gangu sells sweets and small toys that are given at Omatsuri, a traditional street festival.

If you decide to go, it is best to take some friends along in order to share what you buy, as many items are sold only in large quantities. If you feel hungry while you are there, take a break in one of the canteen-like restaurants. A trip to the wholesale market is not really recommended for late risers, as it is already closing time at two o'clock in the afternoon.

Address 東久留米卸売市場, Higashi-Kurume-Sokubai-Ichiba, Shimo-Sato 5-12-12, Higashi-Kurume-shi, 203–0043 Tokyo, +81 (0) 424 712 231 | **Getting there** Seibu-Ikebukuro Line to Higashi-Kurume, then by bus in the direction of Musashikoganei Station to Nishi-Danchi-Iriguchi, 5-minute walk | **Hours** Mon, Tue, Thu–Sat 6.15am–2pm, Sun 8am–2pm | **Tip** The river Ochiai, which is very close to the wholesale market, is a good place for walking and relaxing.

107 — The World Trade Center

A front-row seat to see the Tokyo Tower

Before you start to deplore the supposed fact that the Japanese allegedly copy everything, including the World Trade Center, you should be aware of the following: there are currently 322 such buildings in 89 countries, including three in Japan alone, all of them members of the World Trade Centers Association and mainly dedicated to promoting international trade. The World Trade Center in Tokyo was built in 1970, and at 162.6 metres was even Japan's tallest skyscraper for a short time.

In addition to offices, conference rooms, shops and restaurants, from the 40th storey of the building at a height of 152 metres there is an observation platform with a 360-degree view of the whole city. Although other lookout points such as Sunshine 60 at 226 metres, the Tokyo Metropolitan Government Building at 202 metres, Roppongi Hills at 229.3 metres, the old Tokyo Tower at 249.6 metres and Tokyo Skytree at 451.2 metres are all much taller than the World Trade Center, it is still worth a visit. On the one hand, you have the wonderful view, advertised as Seaside Top, of Tokyo Bay to the east. No other viewing platform is as close to the coast as that at the World Trade Center. On the other hand, the most famous high-rise in Tokyo looks wonderful from here: the Tokyo Tower, which resembles the Eiffel Tower, with the large Zojo-ji Temple in front of it. There is an interesting view of the tracks of the Shinkansen and the other railways that cut through the north side of the city, and also of the multi-level highway that passes to the southeast of the building.

A visit is recommended not only when conditions are clear, but also on overcast days when you can only see part of the city through the clouds. The best time of day to go is early evening, when the sun sets behind the Tokyo Tower. Then you can simply take a seat and enjoy watching as night slowly falls in Tokyo.

Address 世界貿易センタービル, World Trade Center, Hamamatsucho 2-4-1, Minato-ku, 105–0013 Tokyo | Getting there JR-Yamanote Line and others to Hamamatsucho | Hours Daily 10am–8.30pm | Tip To the west of the rail tracks, about 2-minute walk from the World Trade Center, you can visit the Kyu-Shiba-Rikyu Garden, a landscape garden from the Edo period and a striking contrast to the high-rise buildings around it.

108_ Yamaguchi-Kannon

Like a theme park for adults

Do you like the mystic atmosphere of old temples? If so, Yamaguchi-Kannon is the right place for you. A kannon is an enlightened being that is popularly venerated as a deity. This sacred site was inaugurated in its honour. The official name of the temple is Goanzan-Konjoin. The founder is reported to have been the monk Gyoki, who initiated a classical school of Buddhism and was committed to social projects. More good deeds are attributed to him than a single individual can possibly have achieved in one lifetime.

When Kukai, the founder of the Shingon sect and also a figure who is surrounded by many legends of heroic activities, prayed to the dragon god during a pilgrimage, he discovered a holy spring whose miraculous water could heal peasants who had fallen victim to an epidemic.

Centuries later the samurai prince Yoshisada Nitta came to Yamaguchi-Kannon before setting off to the Kamakura War. He prayed that he might win the battle. The votive letter that he signed on 15 February, 1333 is said to exist still. At the spot where he prayed for victory, a cherry tree was planted to honour him. There is a further reminder of this prince on the site: a wooden horse in a stable. This life-size carving represents his favourite horse.

As you look around the temple site, you will also discover the prayer wheels on the outer wall of the main temple hall and the four 'thousand-armed kannon statues'. A delicate metal statue in the shape of a kannon goddess adorns a well. Graves for aborted or still-born children have been decorated imaginatively by family members.

The lovely, colourful ceiling paintings in the buildings have faded in places, and if you look closely you will realise that some of the buildings themselves are in danger of falling into decay. All of which means that this sacred place exudes, in addition to its exotic atmosphere, the mood of a 'lost place'.

Address 山口観音, Yamaguchi-Kannon, Kami-Yamaguchi 2203, 359–1153 Tokorozawa |
Getting there Seibu-Sayamako Line to Seibu-Kyujo-mae, 6-minute walk | Tip The
Yamaguchi Kannon is the first station on the Sayama Kannon pilgrims' way, which takes in
33 holy sites. Take a walk in beautiful countryside to discover the other 32 temples.

109___ The Yodobashi Church
A symbiosis of religious styles

One of the most modern churches in Japan is situated in Okubo. The building was completed in 1999, on the basis of designs by the architect Akira Inadomi, who studied at an Ivy League school and worked with Walter Gropius.

Inadomi designed the Christian pavilion for the world exhibition in Osaka in 1970. After this achievement, churches became his principal area of work.

His architectural style is characterised by the fact that his works combine Japanese and Western religious ideas. Elements that play a part in Shintoism – simplicity, for example, purity and the spiritualisation of nature – as well as the Christian tradition and its liturgy are taken into account. Inadomi endeavours to make his buildings appear authentic and to avoid anachronism, as architectural presentation can undoubtedly have an influence on the cultural acceptance of a religion.

The Yodobashi Church fulfils these aims. It is impressive in its modern style of expression and in its skilfully balanced degree of boldness. The main assembly room of the building is arranged symmetrically and can accommodate a congregation of 1,500 people. The symbol of the cross appears at the highest point in this space: if you look up, you will see a cross of light at the top of the roof. The four sides of this cross are of equal length and are oriented to the diagonals – a geometrical abstraction that expresses the symbolic universal character of the cross, while at the same time creating a dramatic roof shape. The curved form of the sides of the roof lends great architectural power to the space. Although the supports were made from cast concrete, the clarity of this structure reflects the wooden construction of traditional Japanese architecture. This church demonstrates that religious opposites can be united in an artistic creation.

Address 淀橋教会, Yodobashi Church, Hyakunincho 1-17-8, Shinjuku-ku, 169−0073 Tokyo, www.yodobashi-church.com/new/en | **Getting there** JR-Yamanote Line to Shin-Okubo or JR-Sobu Line to Okubo, 2−3-minute walk in each case | **Tip** In Shin-Okubo you will find a specialist shop, Kyowa, which stocks everything needed for Japanese and Chinese calligraphy at the most favourable prices in Tokyo.

110_ Yookanchan
A galactic experience

When walking through a Japanese entertainment district, you will often encounter signs with the English words 'snack' and 'pub'. These places have little in common with a snack bar or a pub in England, however, as the hospitality offered here is typically Japanese. You don't enter these bars, which are often tiny, only to eat and drink, but also to be spoiled and entertained. The hosts – usually they are women – serve a second drink unasked and engage their guests in small talk.

Among the countless bars of this kind, one stands out particularly: Yookanchan, which is the stage name of its proprietor. He is a 77-year-old comedian, known to many Japanese. Wearing gaudy clothing, with blue hair and glittering, flashing accessories he guides his guests through an unbelievable evening. And it is not only the landlord who seems to have landed from a different planet. The whole interior is crazy in the best sense of the word, an all-round work of art with Yookanchan as master of ceremonies. All of the items that cover the floor, walls and ceiling are in themselves kitsch. But in this quantity and arranged as they are here, they give you the feeling that you are in a dreamland. The visual impression is surpassed by the climax of the evening, when Yookanchan rocks the joint, dancing and singing.

If you go there (booking is required) you should be aware of a few unwritten rules that are not necessarily familiar to non-Japanese. There is no menu. A meal of several courses will be served to you without an order. The choice is limited to the drinks, which are replenished again and again. When you have had the last course on the menu – you will recognise this because this is when Yookanchan's performance ends – you should ask for the bill politely and leave (and be sure to have enough cash with you). You will see the world outside with different eyes.

Address よーかんちゃん, Yookanchan, Negishi 1-2-12, Taito-ku, 110−0003 Tokyo, +81 (0) 338 757 022 | Getting there JR-Yamanote Line to Uguisudani, 3-minute walk | Hours Mon−Sat 7pm−midnight; book in advance | Tip Whereas the area around Yookanchan has one of the highest densities of love-hotels in Tokyo, on the other side of the rail tracks, Kan'ei-ji offers a real contrast. The entire Ueno Park once belonged to this temple, which is still of considerable size and has several notable buildings, such as the pagoda.

111 Zoo of the Continents
See the animals

Ueno Zoo became world-famous thanks to its panda. However, if the animals could decide where they prefer to spend their days, they would probably choose to live in Tama Zoo in Hino, as they have very large compounds there. This zoo, which was opened in 1958, covers an area of more than 52 hectares. It is so large that visitors can hardly see all of it in a single day, and therefore the free shuttle bus at their disposal is an extremely practical measure. On the busiest days of the year, this service is restricted to senior citizens, persons with handicaps and visitors with small children.

Tama Zoo is divided according to geographical areas: there is an African, an Asian and an Australian garden. Each of them is home to animals that are typical of one part of the world. There is also an insect house.

One of the biggest attractions is the lions' compound, through which you can ride in a safari bus and observe the big cats close up. This bus service has recently been suspended, as the lion compound is getting a thorough modernisation. It will probably be reopened in 2019.

A further popular feature is the skywalk. If you are in luck, you will be able to watch the orangutans balancing up there at a dizzying height. The skywalk is 150 metres long, and the rope is suspended 15 metres above the ground. The chimpanzees delight onlookers with displays of their dexterity – they have learned how to open drinks cans that they have bought from dispensing machines. The chimps also have no difficulties in operating a gatchagatcha, a vending machine for toys. Other animals take a more relaxed approach to their day. The koalas are happiest when they are asleep in the branches of eucalyptus trees, whereas the tapirs prefer sunbathing in the mud. The cute lesser pandas are a big hit with children. If you like animals, you will love Tama Zoo.

Address 多摩動物公園, Tama Zoo, Hodokubo 7-1-1, Hino-shi, 191–0042 Tokyo |
Getting there Tama monorail to Tama-Dobutsukoen | **Hours** Tue–Thu 9.30am–5pm
(last admission 4pm)* | **Tip** Keio Rail Land near the zoo entrance is the railway museum
of the Keio Line. An attractive outdoor exhibition was added in 2013.

Notes on Using This Book

Names
You will find the names of the places presented in Japanese characters and, where available, in English, in the information boxes.

Hours
When a public holiday falls on a Sunday in Japan, the following Monday is a holiday (Furiae-Kyujitsu). This happens regularly, as several holidays are not tied to a calendar date and are always a Sunday.
Many institutions such as museums, galleries, and some shops and restaurants, are closed on Mondays. If the Monday is a public holiday, however, they stay open and take their day off on the Tuesday. For the places in this book where this rule applies, you will find an asterisk (*) after the opening hours.

Getting there
We have kept the details short, as there is more than one centre in Tokyo and often many alternative ways of reaching your destination. The search engine HyperDia gives you detailed information about the best connections if you enter your starting point and destination: www.hyperdia.com/en. 'Local' in the information boxes means that not all trains stop at the destination station. Local trains (kakueki) stop at every station.

Storeys in buildings
In Japan the ground floor is counted as the first floor, the (European) first floor is the second floor, and so on. To spare you from converting on the spot, we have adopted the Japanese system.

Websites
When this book went to press, many of the websites named in it were only available in Japanese. During our research, almost all of the people we spoke to assured us that English versions would be following soon.

Eras in Japanese History
Here is a list of the main eras in Japanese history mentioned in this book:

Jomon period	approx. 10,000 – 300 BC
Kofun period (Yamato period)	approx. 300 – 710 AD
Heian period	794 – 1185
Edo period	1603 – 1867
Meiji period	1868 – 1912
Taisho period	1912 – 1926
Showa period	1926 – 1989
Heisei period	since 1989

Finally, a note from the authors
Life in Tokyo changes quickly and it may be that some information in this book soon becomes out of date.
We are pleased to provide you with regular updates on our homepage, https://111-orte-in-tokio.jimdo.com.

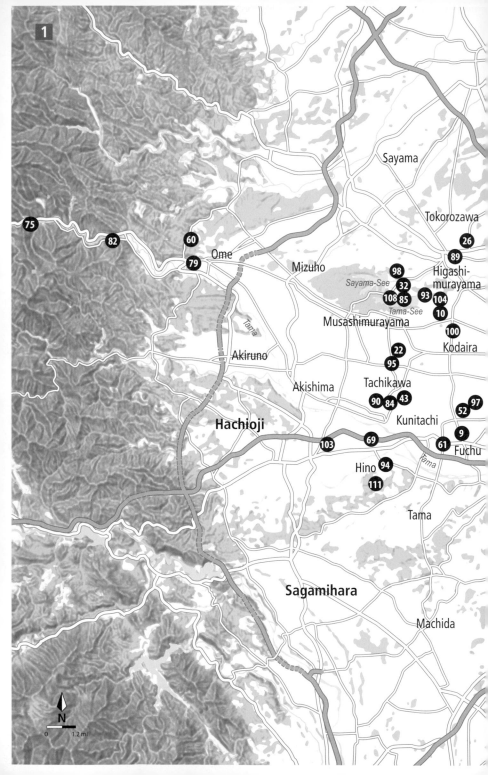

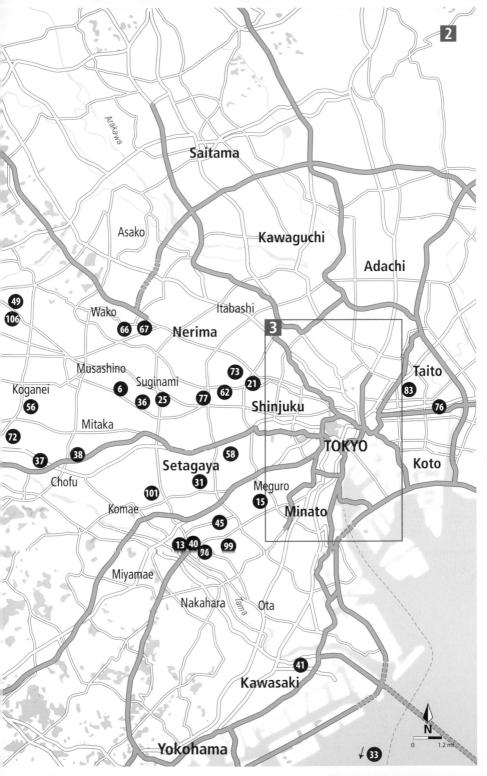

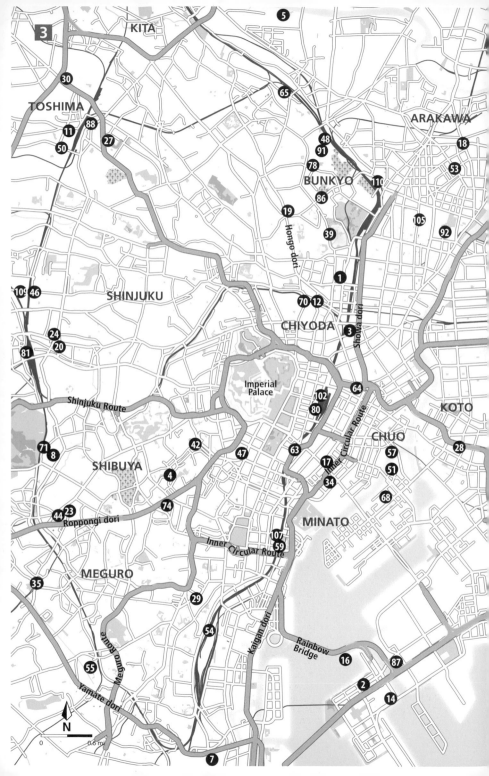

Lucia Jay von Seldeneck,
Carolin Huder, Verena Eidel
**111 PLACES IN BERLIN
THAT YOU SHOULDN'T MISS**
ISBN 978-3-95451-208-9

Rüdiger Liedtke
**111 PLACES IN MUNICH
THAT YOU SHOULDN'T MISS**
ISBN 978-3-95451-222-5

Frank McNally
**111 PLACES IN DUBLIN
THAT YOU SHOULDN'T MISS**
ISBN 978-3-95451-649-0

Rike Wolf
**111 PLACES IN HAMBURG
THAT YOU SHOULDN'T MISS**
ISBN 978-3-95451-234-8

Paul Kohl
**111 PLACES IN BERLIN
ON THE TRAIL OF THE NAZIS**
ISBN 978-3-95451-323-9

Peter Eickhoff
**111 PLACES IN VIENNA
THAT YOU SHOULDN'T MISS**
ISBN 978-3-95451-206-5

Sharon Fernandes
**111 PLACES IN NEW DELHI
THAT YOU MUST NOT MISS**
ISBN 978-3-95451-648-3

Kathrin Bielfeldt,
Raymond Wong, Jürgen Bürger
**111 PLACES IN HONG KONG
THAT YOU SHOULDN'T MISS**
ISBN 978-3-95451-936-1

Gordon Streisand
**111 PLACES IN MIAMI
AND THE KEYS
THAT YOU MUST NOT MISS**
ISBN 978-3-95451-644-5

Dirk Engelhardt
**111 PLACES IN BARCELONA
THAT YOU MUST NOT MISS**
ISBN 978-3-95451-353-6

Rüdiger Liedtke
**111 PLACES ON MALLORCA
THAT YOU SHOULDN'T MISS**
ISBN 978-3-95451-281-2

Marcus X. Schmid
**111 PLACES IN ISTANBUL
THAT YOU MUST NOT MISS**
ISBN 978-3-95451-423-6

Stefan Spath
**111 PLACES IN SALZBURG
THAT YOU SHOULDN'T MISS**
ISBN 978-3-95451-230-0

Ralf Nestmeyer
**111 PLACES IN PROVENCE
THAT YOU MUST NOT MISS**
ISBN 978-3-95451-422-9

Christiane Bröcker,
Babette Schröder
**111 PLACES IN STOCKHOLM
THAT YOU MUST NOT MISS**
ISBN 978-3-95451-459-5

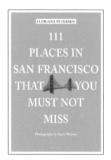

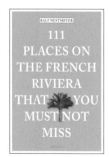

Matěj Černý, Marie Peřinová
**111 PLACES IN PRAGUE
THAT YOU SHOULDN'T MISS**
ISBN 978-3-7408-0144-1

Floriana Petersen, Steve Werney
**111 PLACES IN SAN FRANCISCO
THAT YOU MUST NOT MISS**
ISBN 978-3-95451-609-4

Ralf Nestmeyer
**111 PLACES ON THE
FRENCH RIVIERA
THAT YOU MUST NOT MISS**
ISBN 978-3-95451-612-4

Gerd Wolfgang Sievers
**111 PLACES IN VENICE
THAT YOU MUST NOT MISS**
ISBN 978-3-95451-460-1

Petra Sophia Zimmermann
**111 PLACES IN VERONA
AND LAKE GARDA THAT
YOU MUST NOT MISS**
ISBN 978-3-95451-611-7

Rüdiger Liedtke,
Laszlo Trankovits
**111 PLACES IN CAPE TOWN
THAT YOU MUST NOT MISS**
ISBN 978-3-95451-610-0

Gillian Tait
**111 PLACES IN EDINBURGH
THAT YOU SHOULDN'T MISS**
ISBN 978-3-95451-883-8

Laurel Moglen, Julia Posey
**111 PLACES IN LOS ANGELES
THAT YOU SHOULDN'T MISS**
ISBN 978-3-95451-884-5

Giulia Castelli Gattinara,
Mario Verin
**111 PLACES IN MILAN
THAT YOU MUST NOT MISS**
ISBN 978-3-95451-331-4

John Sykes
**111 PLACES IN LONDON
THAT YOU SHOULDN'T MISS**
ISBN 978-3-95451-346-8

Julian Treuherz,
Peter de Figueiredo
**111 PLACES IN LIVERPOOL
THAT YOU SHOULDN'T MISS**
ISBN 978-3-95451-769-5

Jo-Anne Elikann
**111 PLACES IN NEW YORK
THAT YOU MUST NOT MISS**
ISBN 978-3-95451-052-8

Acknowledgements

We would like to express our gratitude to everyone who has helped us with tips, suggestions and constructive criticism during this project and say thank you for the great support we received from the people behind the places presented in this book.

The authors

Christine Izeki, born in Hamburg in 1966, read Japanese, Indian and German Studies at university in Hamburg and Fukui, and has worked as a journalist in Japan since 1998.

Björn Neumann was born in Kiel in 1969. He read Japanese and Korean Studies in Hamburg and Fukui. Since 2004 he has worked as a German editor and photographer in Tokyo.

Shoko Kinoshita – *Research and "general drudgery"*

Shoko Kinoshita is a translator and tour guide. She has been providing research support to the author team for many years and manages again and again to open doors, even the most resistant ones. It is her hobby to seek out places that have not yet been discovered by everyone else.